Math Problem-Solving Sieck

Brain Teasers

Author:

Sylvia J. Connolly

W9-BZV-916

Introduction

Learning and using problem-solving strategies should be approached by using ideas that make sense to the learner. Abstract concepts practiced without meaning are sometimes fruitless for many students. The problems in this book are meant to provide an atmosphere of problem-solving that allows the student to see the practicality and fun of mathematics.

It is suggested that you use *Math Problem-Solving Brain Teasers* to create interesting classroom projects or as a supplemental tool for students who need more than the curriculum offers. If you or a student can think of a way to extend an exercise or change it, feel free to do so.

Use the information on page three to teach students how to organize for solving problems. Each student should have a plan as to how he or she will solve the problem. Showing steps and collecting necessary data are ways to approach each exercise. Many of these problems can be completed with other students. Analyzing and comparing work makes it possible for students to "see" what good work might look like. If none of your students are able to produce a reasonable response, formulate one yourself and use it as a model of good work. Students must see, touch, and understand in order to learn. Students do not learn when they keep repeating failure. Ensure success by making certain that all work is complete and the exercise is easy to understand for the reader. Students should produce papers that can be understood by anyone who reads them.

As the exercises in this book are completed, have the students save their papers to use as references or models for upcoming activities in which similar problem-solving strategies are employed. In addition, if references are made to previous exercises, those exercises will be available. This book should be used to supplement the textbook with activities that encourage students to expand their thinking. The exercises serve as a springboard from which you as the teacher can create additional problem-solving activities to engage the class.

Contributing Author/Editor:

Barbara M. Wally, M.S.

Teacher Created Materials, Inc.

6421 Industry Way

Westminster, CA 92683

©*1999 Teacher Created Materials, Inc.*

Made in U.S.A.

ISBN-1-57690-219-6

Graphic Illustrator:
James Edward Grace
Illustrator:
Howard Chaney
Cover Artist:
Larry Bauer
Chris Macabitas

Table of Contents

How to Solve Math Problems

There is no one way to solve a math problem. In fact, the teacher's way and the student's way might be different. This is where communication enters the picture. "Can you explain your way so that I may understand how you arrived at your answer?" Answering back, "I don't know, I just got the answer," is not good enough. Regardless of the way in which a problem is solved, the student needs to show his or her thinking. In this way, an error in one of the problem-solving steps can be easily identified. Good communication is clear communication.

Before students begin the exercises in this book, present the following information as one way students can organize their thoughts.

How to Organize Your Thoughts

1. Write down the question in your own words. You can often misinterpret or misunderstand the problem because you were not clear about the question. It is important to understand what is being asked before you can give the answer. Make certain that you understand all the words before you start. Ask questions. Use a dictionary or math reference book.

2. Show all steps. Show *how* you get to each step. Assume that someone outside your class is going to read this and that person must understand your thinking without knowing you. Ask other students to look at your steps to see if they understand. When you show steps, use diagrams, charts, and pictures where needed. Use graphics wherever possible to help you solve the problem.

3. Make certain your answer is clearly stated and, if possible, underline it. If the answer should be stated in some form of measurement, write the value next to the number. For example, if the numerical answer to a problem is 100, and you were asked to find a length in centimeters, express the response as 100 cm, or 100 centimeters.

There are always exceptions to the above. However, just make certain you are communicating as best you can.

The teacher information pages (4, 5, 16, 17, 25–27, 53, 54, 63, 64, 70, 71) correspond to the exercise pages in the sections. Where applicable, teacher notes or information that may be helpful to the students' understanding of the exercises are provided. For easy reference, the exercise page number and title of the exercise are given.

Note: Where possible, metric conversions have been provided. If metric measurement is not given, add or substitute the metric conversion information before reproducing a page.

Teacher Pages: Time Problems

In this section, students will experience hands-on activities and use the results to solve time problems.

Page 6: It's About Time

Students need to see the relationship between different expressions for time and understand how to use common equivalents. For example, 365 days is commonly used as the equivalent of one year. This is not a precise measurement. The calendar currently used throughout the world contains an extra day every fourth year to compensate. Ask some students to research the astronomical basis for the calendar, or the various calendars that have been used throughout history, and present their findings to the class. Students who need assistance with the equivalents may consult the table provided.

Page 7: Behave Yourself

Students will ask you all sorts of questions on this one. If you want to control the study, make everything uniform. If you want the students to explore a bit on their own, tell them to create another study. They will need to decide the subjects and tasks to be used. Remind them that consistency is important.

Page 8: Where's the Fire?

You may wish to add a challenge to this activity by including some stop signs, traffic lights, and one-way street signs before reproducing the map.

Page 9: Find the Fastest Way

Although the shortest distance between two points is a straight line, in real life a number of other factors must be considered, including areas of traffic congestion, one-way streets, etc. The shortest way may not be the fastest way. The means of transportation must also be considered in this problem. Do the students walk, ride a school bus, ride a bike, or are they driven by a parent? If alternative routes are available, an interesting discussion might focus on the fact that taking a particular route to a familiar place becomes habitual for some people.

Page 10: Going the Distance

This is a physics exercise. Have the students measure the angles carefully. They are measuring speed or velocity which is expressed as distance divided by time or distance per time. If possible, compare their results with miles per hour.

Page 11: Timemasters

You may choose the tasks or have the students do this. Sometimes it is just as easy to write the time you start and the time you finish, depending on the task. If you have students working in groups, you might ask them to combine their graphs by using different colors. You could also make a graph with the average of all the students and ask them to put their graph with a different color on the copy. This encourages some interesting discussions.

Teacher Pages: Time Problems (cont.)

Page 12: The Competitive Spirit

The time study described shows how motivation and competition make students perform differently. Students who "see" others perform somehow find more energy.

Page 13: What Time Is It?

Time is related to this motion. Discuss the mathematical connection to time as well. As students make their sundials, they should discover that one hour equals 15°. When sundials are complete and set up as directed, the string should be aligned so that it points approximately north.

Page 14: The Swinging Pendulum

Measuring the angle is a bit of a challenge. You can do this exercise outside on the playground using swings. Measuring the angle here is tricky, but it can be done. Have students research the pendulum clock or clocks in general. It is interesting to learn the history of man's fascination with measuring time.

Page 15: Water Clock

For this activity, students can use the space provided on page 15 or you can have the students write this up on a problem-solving data sheet similar to the sample below. On the form, the student describes the problem to be solved, explains the procedure he or she used to solve it, shows the results, and presents his or her conclusion (solution).

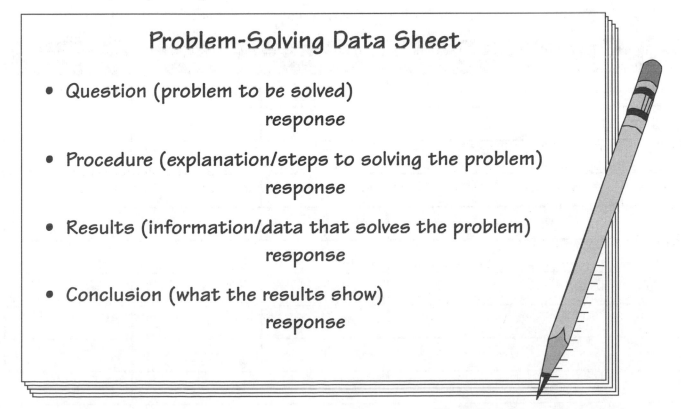

Problem-Solving Data Sheet

- **Question (problem to be solved)**

    response

- **Procedure (explanation/steps to solving the problem)**

    response

- **Results (information/data that solves the problem)**

    response

- **Conclusion (what the results show)**

    response

It's About Time

Time is counted as years, months, weeks, and days. It can be further divided into hours, minutes, and seconds. Calculate how long you have been alive in terms of these units. If necessary, refer to the table of time equivalencies. Then determine how you spend a 24-hour day. How much time do you spend sleeping, eating, watching TV, playing, studying, traveling, etc? Show the results in a pie chart. Record your results in the chart at the bottom of the page.

Table of Time Equivalencies

	Month	Weeks	Days	Hours	Minutes	Seconds
Year	12	52	365	8,760	525,600	31,536,000
Month		4	30 (avg.)	720	432,00	2,592,000
Week			7	168	10,080	604,800
Day				24	1,440	86,400
Hour					60	3,600
Minute						60

Present age: _____ **years** _____ **months** _____ **weeks** _____ **days**

My 24-hour Day

Activity	Hours	Minutes	Seconds

Behave Yourself

Psychologists study behavior. They are very interested in how long it takes an animal or a human to change in some way.

The following activity involves the study of human behavior. You will need a clock or watch with a second hand or a stopwatch. Ask five people to help you with your study. In this activity, you will observe your problem-solving subjects performing several tasks. For the first task, make a complicated math problem. Time how long it takes each subject to complete it correctly. For the second task, mix up the letters of a long word and time how long it takes each person to find the word. For the third task, ask each subject to hum the same short song, like "Happy Birthday" or "Row Your Boat." Time this. Use the chart below to record your results. Write a conclusion on the back of this paper.

Task 1

Problem:

Results:

subject 1 _____

subject 2 _____

subject 3 _____

subject 4 _____

subject 5 _____

Task 2

Mixed-up Word:

Results:

subject 1 _____

subject 2 _____

subject 3 _____

subject 4 _____

subject 5 _____

Task 3

Song Chosen:

Results:

subject 1 _____

subject 2 _____

subject 3 _____

subject 4 _____

subject 5 _____

Where's the Fire?

Firefighters have to know the neighborhood streets. They have to know the quickest way to get to a fire. The map below shows a section of a small town. It shows the fire station and a home which is on fire. Determine three different ways to get to the fire. Choose the one that seems to be the best route. On the back of this paper, tell why you made this choice.

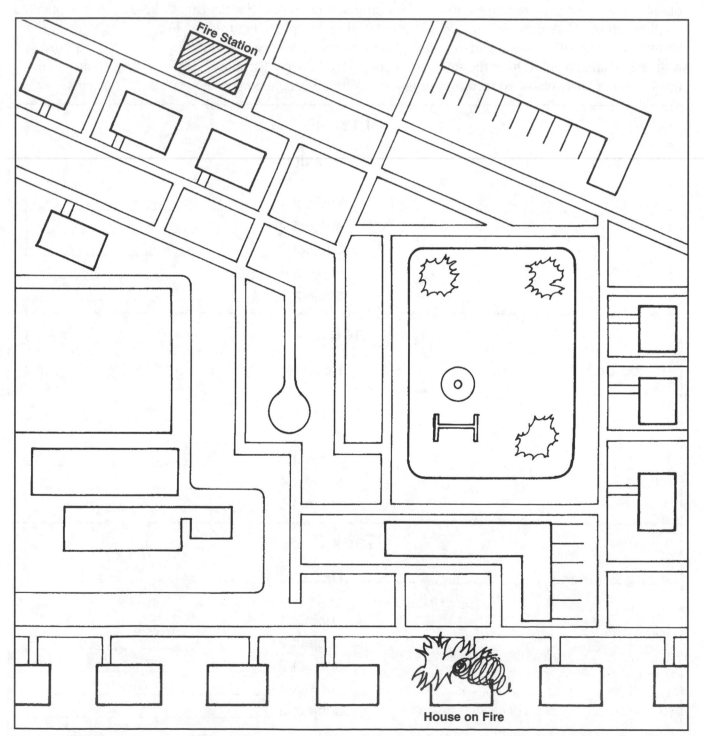

Find the Fastest Way

The map below shows a section of a town. Begin at the location marked "house," and use a colored pencil to draw the shortest route you could take to walk from your home to school and from your home to the grocery store. With a different colored pencil, trace the shortest routes between the points if you were to drive.

Use the scale below the map to determine the distances traveled. The average person walks at a rate of 2 mph (3.2 km/hr), and in this city the speed limit for cars is 30 mph (48 km/hr). **Note:** Add two minutes to your time for every traffic light (marked by an X) you encounter on your route. On the back of this paper, show your calculations and write why you chose these routes.

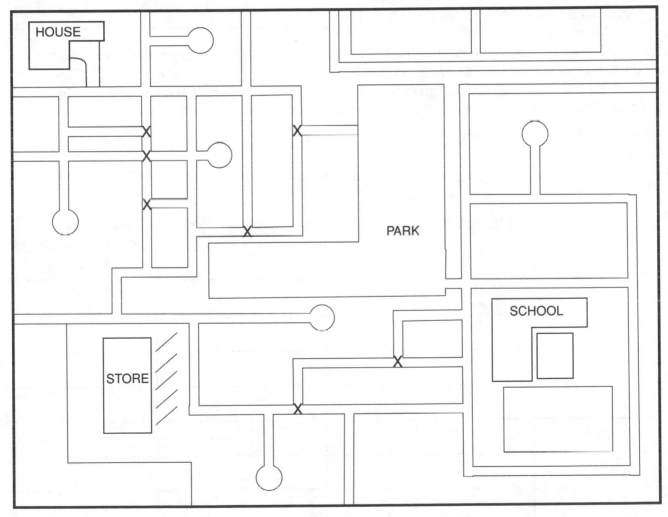

Scale: 1" = .5 mi.   (2.54 cm = .8 km)

Challenge

Find a map of your community, and trace the routes you travel on a regular or daily basis. Measure them and use the map scale to determine the number of miles traveled. Time yourself as you follow the route. Find and explore as many new routes as you can. Be sure to include your means of transportation. Write a conclusion based on the information you collected.

Going the Distance

How are time, distance, and rate of speed related? To find the answer you will need books, tape, a toy car, a long board, a protractor, and a stopwatch or watch with a second hand. For this problem, you will work with time, distance, and rate of speed of an object.

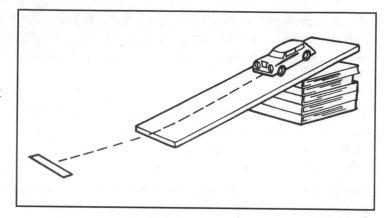

Use the books to elevate one end of the board to create an inclined plane. Use tape to mark off a specific distance on the ground from the end of the board. Add this distance to the length of the board to find the total distance the toy car travels as it moves down the plane onto the ground. Keep this distance the same. Start the car at the top of the inclined plane (board). Time how long it takes for the car to reach the finish line. Do this 10 times, varying the angle of the inclined board each time, while keeping the distance the car travels the same for each trial.

Use the chart below to show the results of each trial in terms of feet (stays the same) per second (this varies).

Data Chart

Trial	Angle	Distance	Time	Distance ÷ Time	Results of column 5 (in feet per second)
1					
2					
3					
4					
5					
6					
7					
8					
9					
10					

Taskmasters

You are sometimes asked to do several tasks at home or at school that take time. How can you best organize your day to accomplish these tasks? For this activity, you will determine the time it takes to complete various tasks and then use this data to plan the best way to carry out your tasks.

1. Decide what tasks can be timed. Make a list of six tasks.
2. Measure the time it takes to complete those tasks. Do this several times. Find the average.
3. Complete the "Task Versus Time" bar graph below.
4. Use your graph results to help you plan how to complete your tasks most efficiently. Write your solution on the back of this paper.

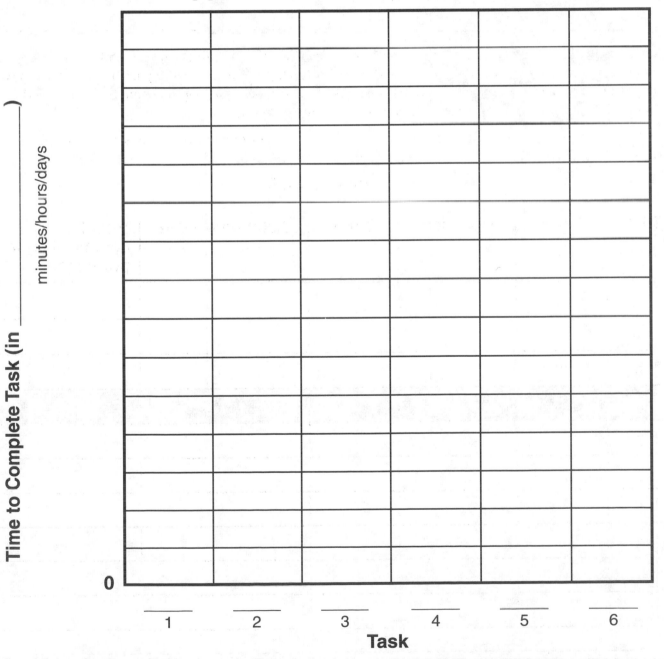

Task

The Competitive Spirit

Does competition affect results? To find out, you will need a stopwatch, a yard or playground area, and three to five friends. Mark off five parallel start-to-finish lanes of equal distance on the ground. (Choose a reasonable distance for walking or running.) Have each participant individually speedwalk from the starting line to the finishing line. Time each person and record the time on a chart below. Make extra copies of this page and perform a second test for running and a third test for walking. Follow the same procedures to time the participants as they complete the tasks simultaneously.

Look at your results. What is your conclusion? How could the results of this activity be used to help solve a problem that a competitor or team might have?

Name	Individual Results	Group Results

Conclusion

What Time Is It?

For this activity, you will make a string sundial and calibrate it to tell time over a 12-hour period (from 6 A.M. to 6 P.M.). You will need a 7" x 9" (18 cm x 22 cm) piece of heavy paper, a pencil, a ruler, a protractor, and a 12" (30 cm) piece of string.

Use your ruler to make a line ½" (1.3 cm) from one of the short ends of the paper. Center your protractor on this line, as shown. Mark the 6 A.M., noon, and 6 P.M. times on the paper as shown on the illustration.

Your problem is to figure out how to mark the hours on the paper so you can use these as hour "hands" on your completed sundial. Once you have determined the hour markings, fold your paper in half lengthwise, making a 90° angle (see illustration). Attach the string at the midpoint of the ½" (1.3 cm) line and at the midpoint of the opposite end of the paper, as shown. (Adjust the length of the string so that the angle matches the latitude angle where you live.) Test your string sundial by placing it on a flat area in the sun. Adjust it so that the shadow cast by the string lines up with the hour angle of the current time. How does it work? Write the problems you encountered and how you solved them.

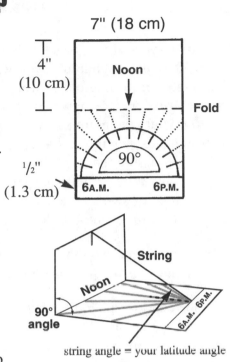

Sundial

 Problems

_____

_____

_____

_____

 Solutions

_____

_____

_____

_____

The Swinging Pendulum

For this activity you will try to solve the mystery of the pendulum. To make a pendulum, you will need a length of string, a weight for the end of the string, a place from which to suspend the string, and a stopwatch or watch with a second hand. Set up your pendulum as shown in the illustration. Pull the weighted string upward as shown. Hold the string in this position. Measure the angle formed by the new position and the pendulum at rest. Set your pendulum in motion. Now, count the number of swings the pendulum makes in a given time (20 seconds, for example). Record your answer.

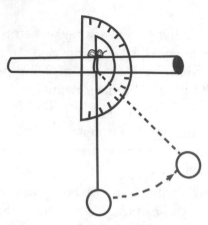

Repeat the experiment two more times. Change the angle each time. Measure the angle and count the number of swings, using the same amount of time as in the first trial.

Complete the chart to show the results for all three pendulums. Use what you discovered to think of a way to make a pendulum that would work as a clock. Write your ideas on the lines provided. Try to solve this problem by testing your ideas.

Trials	1	2	3
Angle			
Number of swings per _____			

_____

_____

_____

_____

_____

_____

_____

_____

_____

Water Clock

Can you make a clock using water? To find the solution, you will need several plastic cups, a container to use as a collecting pan, water, and a timer (stopwatch or watch with a second hand). Use a pencil point, straight pin, or a similar sharp point to puncture a hole in one of the cups so that the hole allows the water to drip at a constant rate. (Be careful when using or storing any sharp objects you may choose for this activity.) Fill the cup with water and immediately place the container beneath it. Use the timer to count the number of drops that fall in a given time.

 Problem: Design a plastic-cup water clock that can be used to measure time.

In the space below, write your plan to solve this problem and then draw and label a picture of what you did to find the solution.

Plan: _____

_____

_____

_____

_____

_____

_____

Work Space

Teacher Pages: Spatial Relationships

Page 18: Polygons and Axioms

Students may find the section areas in a variety of ways. For example, the area of section E (64 cm²) can be found by subtracting the area of A (8 cm²) from the area of one-half the square (72 cm²). Section B and section C are congruent. To find the area of B (30), students could subtract the area of D (12 cm²) from the area of 72 cm² (the area of B + C + D), and then divide that difference in half.

Solution: Area of square (sections A + B + C + D + E) = 144 cm². (Section areas in square centimeters: A = 8, B = 30, C = 30, D = 12, E = 64)

This activity can be extended by using other polygonal shapes. Encourage students to create their own polygon puzzles by cutting different polygons into smaller pieces and reassembling them into new shapes.

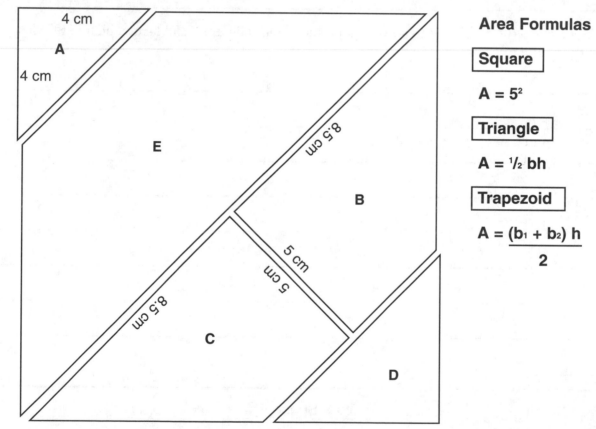

Area Formulas

Square

$A = 5^2$

Triangle

$A = \frac{1}{2} bh$

Trapezoid

$$A = \frac{(b_1 + b_2)\, h}{2}$$

Page 19: Captured Space: A Game

A grid is used for this game. The points of intersection are the end points of the lines. As a variation, have the students draw their lines from the midpoint of one printed line to an adjacent midpoint. The captured spaces will be equilateral triangles.

Page 20: Captured Regions

This game is for the student who likes intricate games and who has the patience to develop strategies. It may not appeal to students who like to hurry. The rules may be modified or simplified to meet the needs and abilities of the class. For example, limit the number of regions to five each, with a total numeric value of 25. Ask the students to suggest rules.

Teacher Pages: Spatial Relationships (cont.)

Page 21: Billiards Math

Have students use their protractors to create the 45°
angles. Note that the figures created by the ball's path
are squares and isosceles right triangles. After the
students have drawn the path for each example, help
them establish the numerical solution: the number of
hits equals the sum of the length and width minus two.
Ask the students to create their own problems to test
the formula. Remember that the measurements of the
sides must be whole numbers.

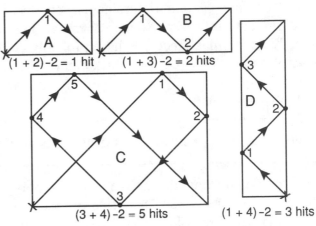

Page 22: Coins in a Triangle

Encourage students to do this with a minimum of moves. (The fewest number of moves = 3). Ask the
students to draw diagrams that show each step. This is good practice for any work done in
mathematics.

Page 23: Networks

Review the definition of vertices as points in a plane. In a network, they are termed "odd" or "even,"
depending on the number of line segments that converge on the point. By tracing the figures, the
students will discover that a traceable network is possible if the figure has only two odd vertices and
impossible with more than two odd vertices. Networks are not limited to connecting locations on a
map. The human circulatory system, computers, and electronics are examples of physical networks.

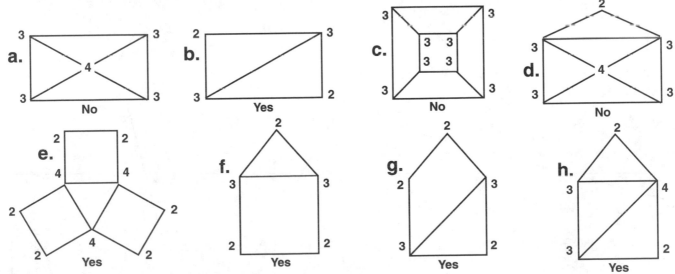

Page 24: Three-D Tic-Tac-Toe

This game was named by students who played it in math contests. Students can explore and develop
strategies so that they can win. Have students play each other only once. This allows them to test their
strategies against different opponents and helps them create new approaches. This is also an excellent
exercise for older students to teach younger students.

Polygons and Axioms

In order to solve geometric problems, some general principles are used. *Axioms*, at one time called "self-evident truths," are basic mathematical principles. There are several axioms with which you may already be familiar, since you have probably performed mathematical operations using them. Think of a situation in which you used this axiom: "If equals are added to equals, the sums are equal."

Here is another axiom:

> **The whole is greater than any of its parts, and it is equal to the sum of all of its parts.**

Can you demonstrate this axiom using the polygons below? Cut out the polygons and arrange them so that they form a square. Then, find the necessary areas to show that this axiom is correct. To help you get started, the area of section D has already been calculated (D = 12 cm²).

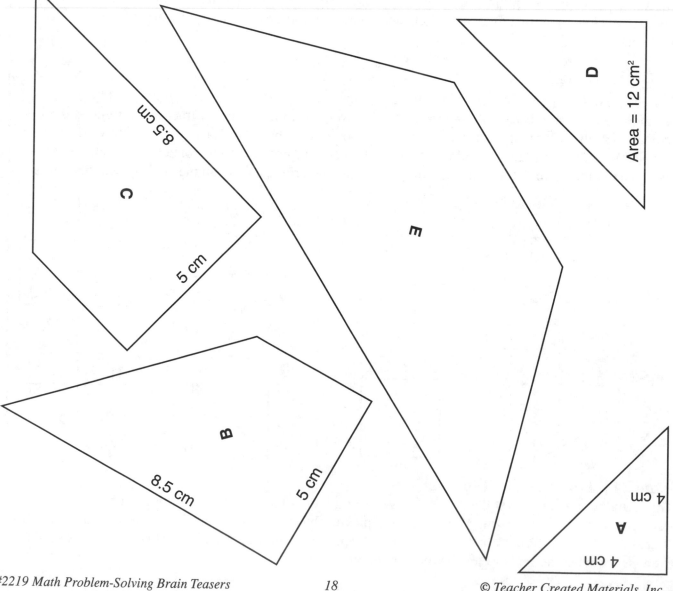

Captured Space: A Game

This game can be played with two or more players. Players take turns drawing a line from one point to an adjacent point. The goal is to draw the last line forming a square. The player who completes the square puts his or her initials inside the square and then gets another turn. The game is played until the page is filled or time is up. The person with the most squares wins the game.

a. Turn one, player one: point to point

b. Turn two, player two: makes a half box

c. Turn three, player one: makes three sides of a box

d. Turn four, player two: makes a complete box, puts in initials, makes another line

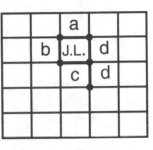

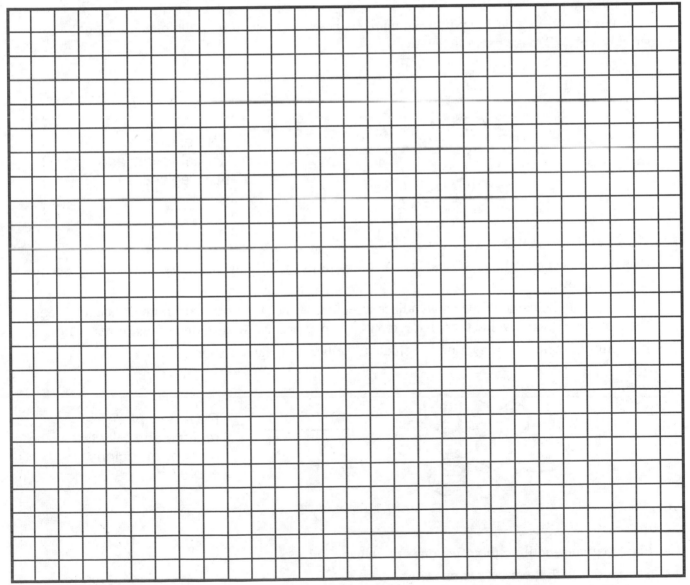

Captured Regions

This game is for two people only. Each player takes a colored pen and draws a region which must be adjacent to the other regions. Do this ten times each. See the example below.

Players build regions that are adjacent to other regions.

Assign values to your regions by putting in numbers between 1 and 100. Each player may use a number only once. See the example below.

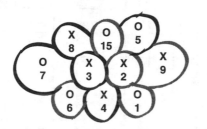

Players assign numerical values and identify regions.

How to Play the Game

- Players are designated by "X" and "O" and take turns identifying and marking regions. (See the example above.)

- A region may be captured when an adjacent region, or the sum of two or more adjacent regions, has a higher numeric value than that region. The player must start in one of his or her regions.

- In capturing regions, a player may include his or her designated regions.

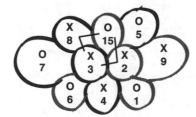

Players capture regions and tally the number of regions captured.

- Play continues until no more regions can be captured.
- The person with the most regions wins.

Billiards Math

Billiards is the name given to a group of indoor games played on a rectangular table. The most common billiard games are snooker, pool, and carom billiards. The standard size of a table is 5 feet by 10 feet (ratio 1:2), with some slight variations. Although the rules vary with the type of billiards played, the object is to hit the balls in a specific way in order to score points. In many games, the object is to follow specific game rules and hit balls into pockets. Billiards is very mathematical, especially regarding the positioning of the ball as it is hit and travels across the table. On a pool table whose sides are whole number ratios, if you hit a ball at a 45° angle from a side of that table at one

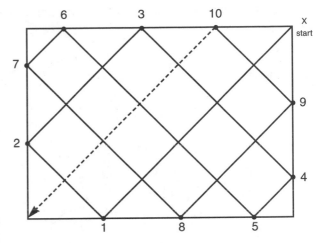

of the integral (whole number) points, the ball will end up in the corner pocket after hitting the sides a certain number of times. The diagram to the right shows how many hits (10) would occur if the table sides were in the ratio 7:5.

How many hits would occur if the table sides were in the following ratios? You will need a protractor for this activity. Show the path a ball would take for each of the following tables. (Note: Begin at the spot marked X.) Mark the hits as shown in the sample diagram. Then, on the back of this paper, draw two more tables and indicate how many hits would occur before the ball falls into a pocket.

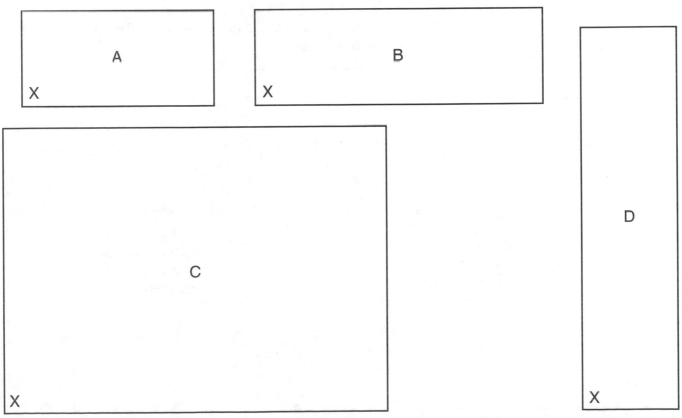

Coins in a Triangle

Take 10 coins and make a triangle with each coin touching at least two other coins. See Example A.

Example A

Example B

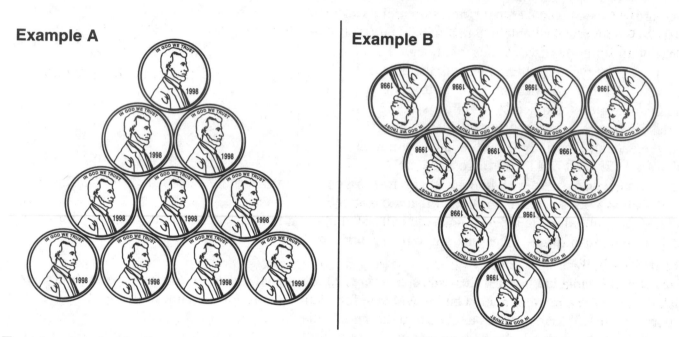

Turn the triangle of coins upside down, as in Example B, by sliding each coin one at a time to a new location so that it touches two other coins.

Use the space below to illustrate each move you make to create the inverse pattern. Try to do this with the fewest number of moves. How many moves did you make?

Networks

The Konigsberg bridge problem is a classic problem. There is a river with two islands and seven bridges in Germany. Is it possible to take a Sunday stroll and cross each bridge only once? Leonhard Euler, a German mathematician, tried to solve this problem by creating networks. He drew a point, or vertex, to represent each land area, and linked the vertices with lines across the bridges. Here is a diagram of the Konigsberg bridge.

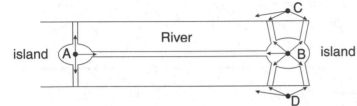

Connectors from Points to Bridges

A = 3	C = 3
B = 5	D = 3

The number of line segments is **odd**.

Can you trace a continuous line over this figure? Make a note of the number of connectors for points A, B, C, and D. The number of line segments for each point is odd. It is impossible to trace a network (in this case, crossing each bridge only once) if the number of connectors radiating from the points is odd for more than two of the points.

See if you can trace your pencil over the following figures without lifting your pencil. (You cannot trace over the same line twice. You can trace over the same point more than once.) For each figure, make a note of the number of connectors converging at each vertex.

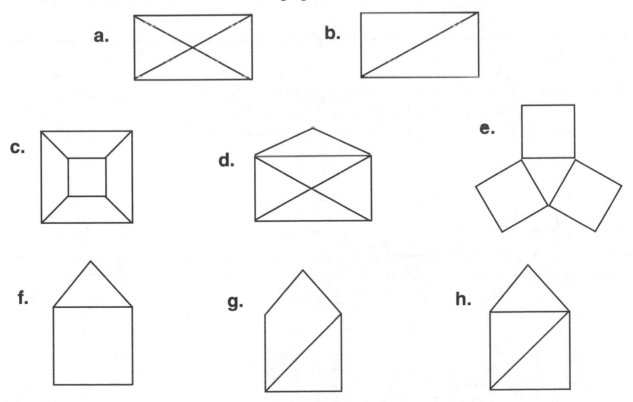

Challenge

Can you redesign the Konigsberg River and the bridges so that a circuit can be made, crossing each bridge only once?

Three-D Tic-Tac-Toe

Doing three-dimensional problems on a two-dimensional surface requires some imagination. For this problem, you will use the rules for tic-tac-toe. Imagine three 3 x 3 grids stacked on top of each other. Grid A is on the top, grid B is in the middle, and grid C is on the bottom. Any three in a row will win the game, but they do not have to be on the same grid (in the same plane). See the example of one way to win. Use the three-dimensional grids below to play several Three-D Tic-Tac-Toe games with a partner.

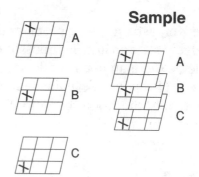

Sample

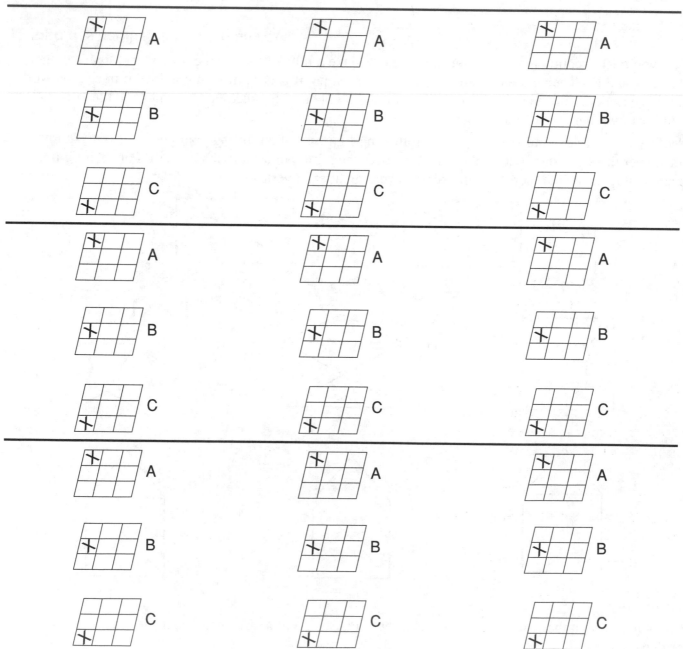

Teacher Pages: Number Relation Problems

Page 28: Writing Numbers

The first recorded use of Hindu-Arabic numbers in Europe was in 976 A.D. The systems that were used before then did not have a concept of or symbol for 0. It is interesting that the Mayans also developed and used the concept of 0. Base 2 is included here because the binary system is the foundation of computer programming where each microswitch may only be on, designated by 1, or off, represented by 0.

Demonstrate using these different systems for calculation with the following exercise. Create simple problems in addition, subtraction, multiplication, and division for the students and challenge them to do each one in each number system. Discuss the results. Which system is the easiest and most versatile?

Problems: $10 + 6 = 16$ $11 - 4 = 7$ $5 \times 3 = 15$

Babylonian

Egyptian

Roman $X + VI = XVI$ $XI - IIII = VII$ $V \times III = XV$

Mayan

Base 2 $1010 + 110 = 10000$ $1011 - 100 = 111$ $101 \times 11 = 1111$

Page 29: Deductive Reasoning

This is the beginning of algebra. You may use symbols to show the pattern. For many students a graphic representation of numbers makes it easier to quantify and see the operation. With advanced students, or as the students become more proficient, you can substitute letters and numbers. Each student should be allowed to try out his or her pattern on another. Have fun with it.

Page 30: Analyzing Sequences

Although sequences are not usually introduced until algebra and calculus, many standardized tests use this type of problem to see if students can recognize patterns. It is important for students to be familiar with how to make patterns with numbers. Include negative numbers in the sequences to see if all the rules hold. Challenge the students to use the method described to solve other problems, like adding the first 10 terms together. There is a very simple shortcut.

Page 31: Geometric Sequences

These sequences are also used in standardized tests and in algebra. Performing an arithmetic operation on the numbers of a sequence is called a series. For example, 1, $^1/_2$, $^1/_4$, $^1/_8$, . . . is a sequence, but $1 + ^1/_2 + ^1/_4 + ^1/_8 + . . .$ is a series. The sequence 0, 0, 0, . . . is called the zero series and is unique because it is both arithmetic and geometric. Zero has many interesting and singular properties. The common ratios on page 31 are as follows: **1.** 5, **2.** $^1/_5$, **3.** $^1/_2$, **4.** -3, **5.** 3, **6.** $^1/_3$ **7.** -2, **8.** -1, **9.** $^2/_3$, **10.** 5.

Teacher Pages: Number Relation Problems (cont.)

Page 32: Fibonacci Numbers

The Fibonacci sequence is intriguing to mathematicians because it seems to describe properties of objects and events in nature as well as abstract mathematics. Challenge the students to find the Fibonacci sequence in Pascal's Triangle, page 33. It is an interesting phenomenon in that when you add any ten numbers of this sequence, the sum equals the seventh term of the particular sequence times 11. Encourage students to perform other arithmetic operations on Fibonacci numbers and analyze the results. Are they Fibonacci numbers? Have students research and report on Fibonacci. He was an interesting individual and contributed much to western mathematics.

(**First 25 Fibonacci Numbers:** 1, 1, 2, 3, 5, 8, 13, 21, 34, 55, 89, 144, 233, 377, 600, 977, 1577, 2554, 4131, 6685, 10816, 17501, 28317, 45818, 74135)

Challenge Example: 0 + 1 + 1 + 2 + 3 + 5 + 8 + 13 + 21 + 34 + 55 = 143; 13 x 11 = 143

Page 33: Pascal's Probability

Blaise Pascal explored probability, and created an array that can be used to determine the outcome of any particular series of events. You may wish to expand the exploration of probability with applications. Does Pascal's probability always apply?

Page 33 Answers

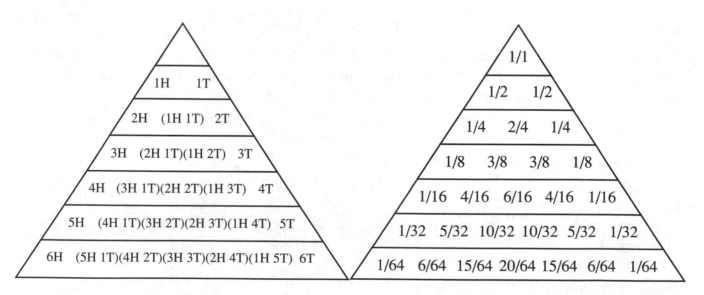

Page 34: Napier's Bones

This activity is a example of someone who created an easier way to solve complex problems. The slide rule is another of Napier's inventions. Showing the students how the abacus works is another way to demonstrate a mechanical method to simplify arithmetic. Ask the students to try to come up with ideas for doing complicated multiplication problems. If the system works, consider it a useful method.

Teacher Pages: Number Relation Problems (cont.)

17	24	1	8	15
23	5	7	14	16
4	6	13	20	22
10	12	19	21	3
11	18	25	2	9

Page 35: Magic Squares

Formulas may be derived from this magic square and used to solve a different array. The center number for any odd magic square is $(n^2 + 1) \div 2$, where n represents the length of one side. Numbers that are equidistant from the center have a sum equal to $n^2 + 1$. Each row, column, and diagonal is equal to $[n(n^2 + 1)] \div 2$. Play with multiples of numbers to preserve the integrity of the square. Books about magic squares are available. The following Web site is devoted to the construction of magic squares: http://www.forum.swarthmore.edu/alejandre/magic.square.html

Page 36: Golf Ball Pyramid

It may be easier for some students to understand pyramid numbers if they actually build the pyramid. If you build a large pyramid with golf balls, experiment to see how many golf balls can be taken away before the pyramid collapses. Note that the solution to the number of golf balls is the sum of the squares of the number of layers in the pyramid. For a 10 x 10 base golf ball pyramid, the number of golf balls equals 385.

Page 37: Sieve of Eratosthenes

This is an excellent computer programming exercise because it is so mechanical. Challenge students to generate the sieve for the first 500 numbers, or have the students make a poster showing the sieve for the first 100 numbers to display and use as a reference chart. The chart on page 37 should show that the following numbers are *not* crossed out: 2, 3, 5, 7, 11, 13, 17, 19, 23, 29, 31, 37, 41, 47, 53, 59, 61, 67, 71, 73, 79, 83, 89, and 97.

Page 38: Numerical Palindromes

Whether they are numbers or letters, palindromes have the unusual quality of being the same when read from left to right as when they are read from right to left. The method given here is one way to generate a numerical palindrome. You may wish to challenge the students to find other ways this number trick can be accomplished. The squares of certain integers also create palindromes. For example, 1 x 1 = 1, 11 x 11 = 121, 111 x 111 = 12321, etc. Does this pattern continue? Challenge students to test the method with other numbers to determine if this will always produce palindromes. If not, what are the limitations? Can the students think of any other ways to produce palindromes?

Page 39: Secret Codes

There are two basic methods used to create secret codes: transposition and substitution. In a transposition code, the letters are scrambled; in a substitution code, each original letter is replaced by a different letter or symbol. The possibilities for encoding a message are endless, especially when computers are used. Let the students challenge each other with their secret messages.

Message: Sending secret messages can be fun. Codes can be made with letters, numbers, or other symbols. To read a message written in a secret code when you do not have a key, determine the frequency of each letter in the message and use the chart to find the letter to substitute.

Writing Numbers

The numbers we use are called Arabic numbers. They were first developed in India and introduced to the rest of the world by Arab traders. This system gained popularity because it was far easier to use than most of the previous number systems. One of the most important concepts that the Arabs helped to introduce was zero. Without zero, our decimal system would not be possible. The following table shows the first 11 numbers in 5 other systems. Note that the ancient Mayans also discovered and used a symbol for zero.

Arabic	1	2	3	4	5	6	7	8	9	10	11
Babylonian	▼	▼▼	▼▼▼	▼▼▼▼	▼▼▼ ▼▼	▼▼▼ ▼▼▼	▼▼▼▼ ▼▼▼	▼▼▼▼ ▼▼▼▼	▼▼▼ ▼▼▼ ▼▼▼	<	<▼
Egyptian	I	II	III	IIII	II III	III III	III IIII	IIII IIII	IIII IIIII	Ω	Ω I
Roman	I	II	III	IV	V	VI	VII	VIII	IX	X	XI
Mayan	○	○○	○○○	○○○○	—	○ —	○○ —	○○○ —	○○○○ —	═	○ ═
Base 2	1	10	11	100	101	110	111	1000	1001	1010	1011

Use the patterns above to extend each system to show the numbers 12 to 25. Can you show how to add, subtract, multiply, and divide in each of these number systems? Illustrate an example for each system.

Arabic	12	13	14	15	16	17	18	19	20	21	22	23	24	25
Babylonian														
Egyptian														
Roman														
Mayan														
Base 2														

Deductive Reasoning

Can you find a pattern of operations that can be used on any number so that the answer is always the same?

Here is one example:

• Choose any numbers.	4	7	9
• Add 5 to each number.	$4 + 5 = 9$	$7 + 5 = 12$	$9 + 5 = 14$
• Double each sum.	$2 \times 9 = 18$	$2 \times 12 = 24$	$2 \times 14 = 28$
• Subtract 4 from each product.	$18 - 4 = 14$	$24 - 4 = 20$	$28 - 4 = 24$
• Divide each result by 2.	$14 \div 2 = 7$	$20 \div 2 = 10$	$24 \div 2 = 12$
• Subtract the original numbers.	$7 - 4 = 3$	$10 - 7 = 3$	$12 - 9 = 3$

Can you write a general rule for the above series of operations? In each step the same operation was done to each number. Use **n** to represent any number, and write the steps as a mathematical sentence or formula.

$$\frac{[(n + 5)\,2] - 4}{2} - n = 3$$

Now try this pattern on your own.

- Choose any three numbers.

- Double each number.

- Add nine to each of the products.

- Add the original number to each number.

- Divide each of the sums by three.

- Add four to each quotient.

- Subtract the original numbers.

What is the result in each case? Can you find the pattern and write it as a formula?

Create your own deductive reasoning problem, and write the pattern as a formula. Ask another student to try it to see if you are correct.

Analyzing Sequences

Sometimes we write numbers that have a particular pattern.

- Here is one: 1, 2, 3, 4, 5. . .   The three dots mean to continue the pattern.

  This is a sequence of numbers that are counting numbers.

- Here is another: 2, 4, 6, 8, 10. . .

  This is the sequence of even numbers.

- Here is one more: 7, 10, 13, 16, 19. . .

  This sequence begins with seven, and each consecutive number is the previous one plus three.

Each of the numbers in a sequence is called a *term*. In the last sequence above, the first term is seven.

Can you find the fiftieth term in each of the above sequences?

The first is easy. All you have to do is count to find that the fiftieth term is 50.

For the second, counting by two gives the answer of 100.

The third is not as easy. You could write out the entire sequence to find the fiftieth term. Is there an easier way?

Analyze the problem deductively to find a pattern.

- The first term is 7 or 7 + (0 x 3).
- The second term is 10 or 7 + (1 x 3).
- The third term is 13 or 7 + (2 x 3).
- The fourth term is 16 or 7 + (3 x 3).
- Apply the formula to find the fiftieth term: 7 + (49 x 3) = 7 + 147 = 154.

What is the forty-third term for this sequence? _____

Check to see if this formula will work for any sequence.

1. Make three arithmetic sequences that are different from the examples above, and write each to its fiftieth term.
2. Circle the forty-first term for each sequence.
3. Now use the formula to find the forty-first term of each sequence.
4. Are the answers the same?

Geometric Sequences

An arithmetic sequence is one in which the same number is added (subtraction is negative addition) to the previous term. A geometric sequence is one in which each new number is the result of multiplying (division is inverse multiplication) the previous term by some number.

Arithmetic Sequence Example: 1, 3, 5, 7. . .

Geometric Sequence Example: 1, 3, 9, 27, 81. . .

The word *term* refers to the numbers.

The *common ratio* is the number by which each term is multiplied to form the next term. In the above geometric sequence, three is the common ratio.

In the sequences below, find the common ratio and do five more terms.

1. 2, 10, 50, _____

2. 3.5, .7, .14 _____

3. 1, $\frac{1}{2}$, $\frac{1}{4}$, _____

4. -1, 3, -9 _____

5. 1.5, 4.5, 13.5 _____

6. 1, $\frac{1}{3}$, $\frac{1}{9}$, _____

7. 2, -4, 8, _____

8. -1, 1, -1, _____

9. $\frac{2}{3}$, $\frac{4}{9}$, $\frac{8}{27}$, _____

10. $\frac{1}{5}$, 1, 5, _____

Now make up your own sequences. Write only the first three terms. Exchange problems with a classmate, and solve each other's sequences for the next three terms and the ratio.

Fibonacci Numbers

Leonardo Fibonacci, also called Leonardo of Pisa, discovered the interesting sequence of numbers that is named for him. Fibonacci lived in the late twelfth century and studied mathematics in India. The numbers of his sequence occur often in nature and in other mathematical concepts. Today this sequence is used in computer programming.

> To find the sequence, start with 0, 1 and add them to find the next number: 0, 1, 1. Now add the previous two for the next term: 0, 1, 1, 2. In writing the sequence, the zero is often left off, since it has no value. The first five terms of the Fibonacci numbers are usually considered to be 1, 1, 2, 3, 5.

Now Try This

Use the information above to write the first 25 terms (starting with the number 1) of the Fibonacci numbers. If you wish, you may continue to write the next 25 terms on the back of this paper.

_____ _____ _____ _____ _____

_____ _____ _____ _____ _____

_____ _____ _____ _____ _____

_____ _____ _____ _____ _____

_____ _____ _____ _____ _____

Challenge

Add the first ten terms. Is the answer 11 times the seventh term? Take any ten consecutive terms in this sequence and add them. Is the result 11 times the seventh term? Show your work below.

Pascal's Probability

Mathematician Blaise Pascal made a study of probability in the seventeenth century. He devised a method that can be used to show all the possible outcomes of an event and calculate the chances of that particular outcome. Pascal's triangle is very useful for all kinds of calculations. Can you see the pattern of the triangle? Add two rows of numbers to it. Write the sum of the numbers in each row. Is there a pattern?

When you flip a coin, the result is either heads or tails. The result is not always the same, and you do not know in advance what the outcome will be for a particular trial. You can, however, predict the probability or odds of a particular outcome. Each time you flip the coin, the probability of it landing heads up is 50 percent. If you flip the coin several times, how many times will it land on heads?

Toss a coin six times and record the results in the chart below. The last column shows the possible results based on the number of tosses.

Trial	Result	Possible Combinations
1	__H __T	H, T
2	__H __T	HH, HT, TT
3	__H __T	HHH, HHT, HTT, TTT
4	__H __T	HHHH, HHHT, HHTT, HTTT, HHHH
5	__H __T	HHHHH, HHHHT, HHHTT, HHTTT, HTTTT, TTTTT
6	__H __T	HHHHHH, HHHHHT, HHHHTT, HHHTTT, HHTTTT, HTTTTT, TTTTTT

On the back of this paper make two triangles. In the first triangle, write the possibilities for the six coin tosses. To find the probability for each coin, use Pascal's triangle. Fill in the your second triangle as follows: use Pascal's numbers as the numerator of a fraction; use the sum of the numbers in the row as the denominator. In any six tosses, how many times can you expect the results to be even, with three heads and three tails?

Napier's Bones

John Napier (1550–1617), a Scotsman, discovered logarithms, which can be used to calculate difficult computations. Napier also invented a set of numbered rods to help merchants with their accounting. These numbered rods were made of ivory and resembled bones, so they were called "Napier's Bones."

Each rod has a number and its multiplication table arranged in the following way:

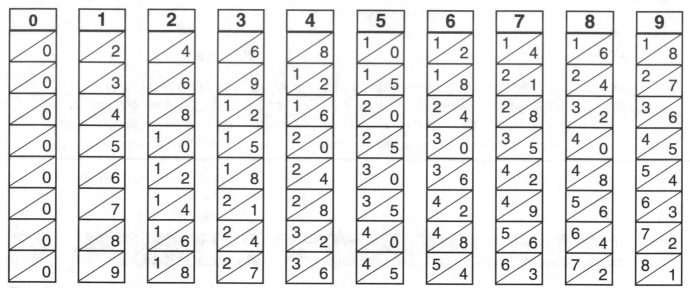

To solve a problem like multiplying 347 by 8, use the rods 3, 4, 7. Put them next to each other. Count down 8 rows, *starting with the number 3*. Write down the top numbers (tens), adding a zero at the end to show that the numerals represent tens. Below these, write down the bottom numbers (ones). Find the sum.

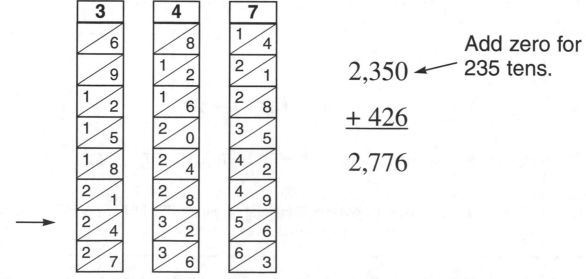

2,350 ← Add zero for 235 tens.

+ 426

2,776

Now Try This

Make your own Napier's Bones with paper. Multiply the following numbers: 346 x 3; 501 x 8; 714 x 5. Can you figure out a way to use Napier's Bones to multiply using double digits? Write your method on the back of this paper.

Magic Squares

A magic square is a square of numbers in which the sum of each row, diagonal, and column is the same. There is much written about magic squares. In the following activity you will discover and use the rules for creating odd magic squares (squares in which the number of boxes on each side is odd).

Here is an odd magic square. Notice that each row, column, and diagonal adds up to the same number—15. There are other observations about the number relationships and design of the magic square as well. Follow the steps below to see how this odd magic square was created. Then, use the information to create a 5 x 5 magic square.

8	1	6
3	5	7
4	9	2

Creating Magic Squares

1. Write the number 1 in the middle box of the top row.

2. Place the next number (2) in the box that is diagonally up (up and to the right). If no box exists there, then the number should occupy the same position (diagonally up from and to the right of its predecessor) in a phantom, or imaginary, square that exists directly below the original square.

3. As you proceed to add numbers in this way, you will eventually come to a box that is already occupied. In this case, place the number directly beneath its predecessor.

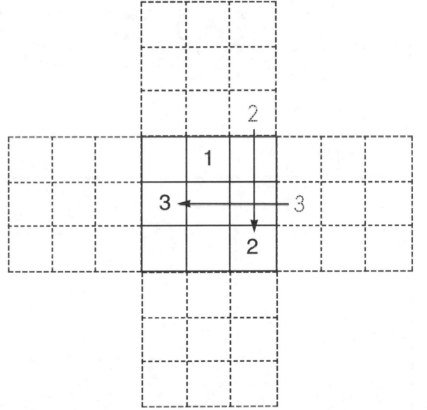

Here are some important formulas to use as guidelines to making an odd magic square and for checking to number placement and relationships within the square. In the formulas below, n = the number of boxes on a given square. (In the square above, for example, n = 3.)

- The numbers range from 1 to n^2
- The magic number (the number that represents the diagonal, column, or row sums) is found by using this formula: $[n(n^2 + 1)] \div 2$.
- Any two numbers (in the same row, diagonal, or column) that are equidistant from the center box have the sum, $n^2 + 1$.
- The number in the center box equals $(n^2 + 1) \div 2$.

Golf Ball Pyramid

The sequence 1, 4, 9, 16, 25, 36. . . is made of "squared" numbers. In it, each of the natural numbers 1, 2, 3, 4, 5, 6, . . . is multiplied by itself, or squared. Now imagine that each one of these numbers is the base of a pyramid, and each pyramid is made of golf balls. If the base is 2 x 2, only one ball fits on the top. This makes 5 golf balls in all. On a base that is 3 x 3, 4 balls fit on top, and one more layer with one ball can be added for a total of 14 balls.

Arrangement of First Two Groups of Golf Balls

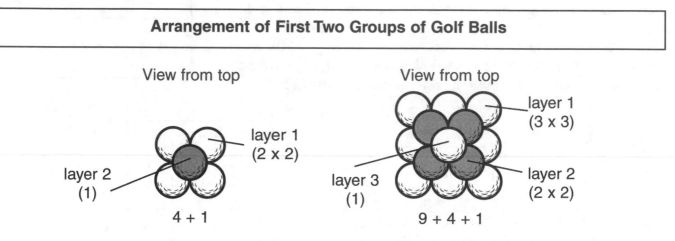

Continue building pyramids, increasing the size of the base according to this pattern. Show your work in the space below.

If a pyramid has a base of 10 x 10 golf balls, what is the total number of golf balls? Can you solve the problem mathematically? Explain your answer.

Sieve of Eratosthenes

The Sieve of Eratosthenes is used to find prime numbers. The definition of a prime number is a number that can only be divided by one and itself. One is not prime. Here is a short version.

1̶	②	③	4̶	⑤	6̶	⑦	8̶	9̶	1̶0̶
⑪	1̶2̶	⑬	1̶4̶	1̶5̶	1̶6̶	⑰	1̶8̶	⑲	2̶0̶
2̶1̶	2̶2̶	㉓	2̶4̶	2̶5̶	2̶6̶	2̶7̶	2̶8̶	㉙	3̶0̶

Steps

1. Cross out the number one.

2. Circle the number two, and cross out multiples of two.

3. Circle the next number, and cross out multiples of that number.

4. Continue until all numbers are circled or crossed out.

You now have a list of all the prime numbers. In the above exercise 2, 3, 5, 7, 11, 13, 17, 19, 23, and 29 are prime.

Make a sieve for the first 100 numbers.

1	2	3	4	5	6	7	8	9	10
11	12	13	14	15	16	17	18	19	20
21	22	23	24	25	26	27	28	29	30
31	32	33	34	35	36	37	38	39	40
41	42	43	44	45	46	47	48	49	50
51	52	53	54	55	56	57	58	59	60
61	62	63	64	65	66	67	68	69	70
71	72	73	74	75	76	77	78	79	80
81	82	83	84	85	86	87	88	89	90
91	92	93	94	95	96	97	98	99	100

Numerical Palindromes

A *palindrome* is a word, phrase, or number that is the same when it is read frontwards or backwards. Words like toot and dad are simple palindromes. "A Toyota" and "Madam, I'm Adam" are examples of phrases that are palindromes. Numbers like 1221 and 576675 are numerical palindromes.

NOON

MOM

12321

401104

DID

The following is a method to generate a numerical palindrome.

1. Start with any four-digit number.   1563

2. Reverse the digits.   3651

3. Add the original number.   1563 + 3651 = 5214

4. Reverse the digits.   4125

5. Add the numbers.   5214 + 4125 = 9339

This is a palindrome!

Do this for six different numbers to test the process. The number of times that you will have to repeat the process of reversing and adding will vary. Can you find another way to produce palindromes?

Secret Codes

Secret messages can be fun. Numbers and letters can be substituted for the original letters in a message. Sometimes there is a key for translation that the sender and receiver both know and use. How can you read a message if you do not have the key?

Some letters occur more frequently than others in words in the English language. The letter E is the most frequent. The table below shows the probability for each letter as a percentage. It was developed by examining and analyzing a great amount of written material.

E	12.7	S	6.5	U	2.9	G	1.5	J	0.2
T	9.3	R	6.3	F	2.6	B	1.4	Z	0.1
O	8.1	H	5.5	M	2.4	V	1.0		
A	7.9	D	3.9	P	2.2	K	0.5		
N	7.2	L	3.8	W	1.8	X	0.2		
I	7.0	C	3.1	Y	1.7	Q	0.2		

Use this information to read the message below. Count the number of times each letter appears in the coded message and list them in decreasing order. Find the total number of letters in the message and calculate the percentage of occurrence of each letter. Now you can compare the occurrence of various letters in the message to the table. Use the information to begin substituting letters. Look for familiar letter patterns as you go, like "th." Common patterns and double letter combinations can provide additional keys.

Hint: *Code letter X = alphabet letter E, code letter W= alphabet letter S*

WXJOKJE / WXRBXQ / IXWWZEXW / RZJ / LX / VTJ.

RMOXW / RZJ / LX / IZOX / DKQP / CXQQXBW / , / JTILXBW / , / MB / MQPXB / WAILMCW.

QM / BXZO / Z / IXWWZEX / DBKQQXJ / KJ / Z / WXRBXQ / RMOX / DPXJ / AMT / OM / JMQ / PZGX / Z / HXA / , / OXQXBIKJX / QPX / VBXNTXJRA / MV / XZRP / CXQQXB / KJ / QPX / IXWWZEX / ZJO / TWX / QPX / RPZBQ / QM / VKJO / QPX / CXQQXB / QM / WTLWQKQTQX.

In the box, create your own code. Write a message and translate it into your code. Trade coded messages with a classmate and decipher them.

Teacher Page: Nature Problems

Many important scientific and mathematical discoveries are the result of observations of patterns in the natural world. Encourage your students to look for naturally occurring numbers and/or quantifiable or measurable events. Inspiration for nature study can be found in *The Case of the Mummified Pigs* by Susan E. Quinlan, Boyd's Mill Press, 1995.

Page 41: Crystal Formations

If you have access to a microscope, show students the geometric formations of crystals in ordinary household compounds. Crystal formations in rocks and minerals, especially geodes, are visible to the naked eye. Have the students use the correct names to identify each formation, and ask them to list the solids they observe in each compound or rock. You may have each student make a complete set of solids or assign one solid to each student or group of students to create a class set. The more careful and accurate the students are in marking and folding the circles to form the sides, the more exact the models will be. Using colored paper or shading the paper circles with colored pencils or crayons will make the display more interesting. Encourage the students' creativity here.

solid	number of sides	shape of one face
tetrahedron	4	triangle
hexahedron	6	square
octahedron	8	equilateral triangle
dodecahedron	12	regular pentagon
icosahedron	20	equilateral triangle

Page 42: Making a Snowflake

This is a curve that is discussed in fractal geometry. Fractal geometry has many recursive patterns. Students can make their own designs if they are so inclined. Remind them to start with one geometric shape and make additions using the same pattern. Precision in measuring and placement is also important here. Fractals may be generated by computers, but it is more interesting and challenging to make your own. Ask the students to look for naturally appearing fractals and record them. Benoit Mandelbrot used the rugged coastline of the British Isles as an example of a fractal. Examine cloud formations and rock formations.

Page 43: Big Foot

Although the ideal situation is to have the students observe animal tracks in the field, research may be substituted. If possible, bring in snowshoes, diving fins, and different kinds of skis. Let the students have fun calculating the sink factors.

Crystal Formations

Crystals grow in the shapes of polyhedrons, or solid geometric shapes with polygon faces. If you look at salt crystals with a powerful magnifying lens or a microscope, you will see cubes and tetrahedrons. Aluminum crystals are octahedrons. Certain minerals also take the shape of crystals. When you cut a geode in half, quartz crystals are revealed.

Cubes, tetrahedrons, octahedrons, dodecahedrons, and icosahedrons are called *Platonic solids*, after Plato, who first described them about 400 B.C. In a regular polyhedron, each side or face is identical to the other faces. The angles of each face are also equal. Although polyhedrons take on many shapes, only the five discovered by Plato are regular polygons.

Look at the pictures of these solids and complete the chart.

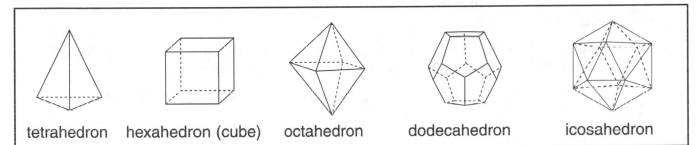

| tetrahedron | hexahedron (cube) | octahedron | dodecahedron | icosahedron |

solid	number of sides	shape of one face
	4	
	6	
	8	
	12	
	20	

Now create models of these solids.

1. Cut a circle with a radius of 2 inches (5 cm) for each face of the polygon you wish to make.
2. Use your protractor and compass to inscribe a regular polygon on each circle.
3. Fold the edges of the circle to create the polygonal faces.
4. Glue the faces together along the folded edges to form the polyhedron. You may position the folded portions of the circles inside the figure for a pristine shape or on the outside if you want a more rugged shape.

Challenge

R. Buckminster Fuller designed and patented the geodesic dome, a building made from polyhedrons. Use your models to determine which polyhedrons can be used in this way, and create a model of a geodesic dome.

Making a Snowflake

Many geometric forms occur in nature. Benoit Mandelbrot made a study of curves he called fractals. One interesting feature of fractals is that they are "self-similiar," which means that some feature of the curve is repeated on a different scale. Self-similarity can be used to create interesting shapes and patterns. High-speed computers allow mathmeticians to explore and create very complex fractal patterns.

Create Your Own Snowflake

1. Draw a large equilateral triangle in the center of a separate piece of paper.

2. Trisect each side of the triangle.

3. Use the middle third of each side as a base for a new equilateral triangle. Erase the bases of the new equilateral triangles.

4. Trisect each side of the newly formed triangles. Construct new equilateral triangles using the middle third of the sides as the bases. Erase the bases of the new triangles.

5. Repeat the process until you cannot create anymore triangles. You have made a snowflake curve.

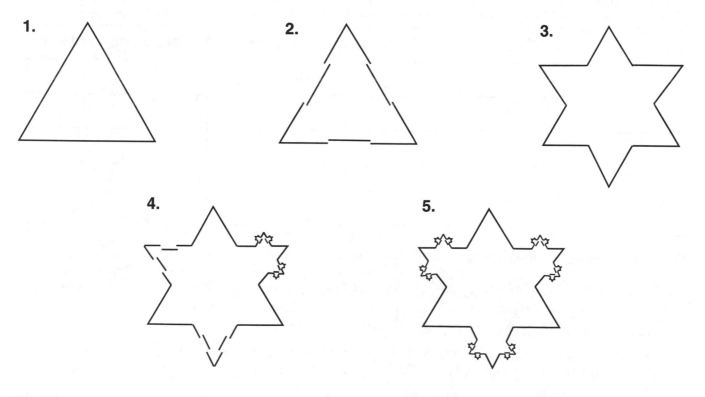

Challenge

Can a fractal be inscribed in the figure? Draw a large equilateral triangle. Bisect each side and inscribe a triangle. Continue the process. Write complete directions for this figure. Choose another equilateral polygon, and follow the above procedure. What is the result?

Big Foot

By observing the tracks left by animals, we can learn about the animals that made them. Birds and certain other animals can walk across a snowy field or muddy plain, leaving only their tracks behind while a person would sink. How is this possible?

The answer lies in the ratio of the bird's weight to the size of its feet. The calculation is called the sink factor and is written as weight (in kilograms) ÷ foot area (in square centimeters). The diagram to the right shows the prints of a snowshoe hare. The two front feet are 20 square centimeters and the two hind feet are 76 square centimeters for a total of 96 square centimeters. A snowshoe hare weighs 1.5 kg, so its sink factor equals 1.5 ÷ 96 or 0.016. A heavier animal with the same size feet would have a larger sink factor, while a lighter animal with the same size feet would have a lower sink factor.

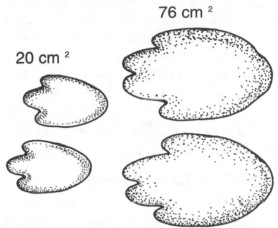

76 cm^2

20 cm^2

weight ÷ total surface area = sink factor
1.5 ÷ 96 = 0.016

Now Try This

Trace your feet on a piece of metric graph paper, and calculate your foot area. In the box below, calculate your sink factor.

Now think of some ways to change your sink factor. Recalculate your sink factor for at least two different kinds of footwear. Which design provides the most favorable (smallest) sink factor ratio? If possible test your selected footwear in the snow. Explain your findings below.

Teacher Pages: Science Problems

Page 46: Distances of the Planets from the Sun

Because of its magnitude, drawing the solar system is not easy. If you have time, have the students create a map of the solar system on the playground. Measure a long piece of string to use as a scale, and mark the position of the planets with tape, or assign a student to stand in the position of each planet. Start by using one inch (or centimeter) to represent 1,000,000 miles. The distances might be greater than your playground or park. Discuss this huge distance. The extremely large numbers here provide an opportunity to introduce the concept of scientific notation. Remind students that any number that ends in a zero is the number times 10. A number ending in two zeros is the number times 100, or 10 to the second power. Challenge students to find the pattern and write the distances of the planets using this system of notation.

Page 47: Matter Matters

You will need ice, a container, and a ruler for this exercise. Students study matter as it changes from one state to another by measuring and comparing solid and liquid volumes. They will have to determine the information and labels to add to the grid on page 47 before graphing their results.

Page 48: Half Full

This problem will challenge students to use known measurements to arrive at an appropriate solution. This can be done as a hands-on task, with students recording their steps as they carefully pour water from one container to another. The graph provided on page 48 can be re-created with pushpins or small nails on a piece of corkboard or corrugated paper. Use string or yarn to show the moves required. Have the students solve the problem twice, beginning once with the five-quart container and once with the seven-quart container. Compare the results. Which requires fewer pourings?

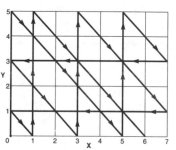

Sample solution: The information in the parentheses below refers to the amount of liquid in the containers. The first number represents the contents of the 12-quart container, the second number represents the contents of the 5-quart container, and the third number represents the contents of the 7-quart container. To follow the plotted points (7- and 5-quart containers) on the graph above, refer to the second and third numbers, y and x, in the parentheses.

1. Fill the 5-quart container. (7, 5, 0)
2. Pour liquid from the 5-quart container into the 7-quart container. (7, 0, 5)
3. Fill the 5-quart container. (2, 5, 5)
4. Pour 2 quarts from the 5-quart container into the 7-quart container. (2, 3, 7)
5. Empty the 7-quart container into the 12-quart container. (9, 3, 0)
6. Empty the 5-quart container into the 7-quart container. (9, 0, 3)
7. Fill the 5-quart container from the 12-quart container. (4, 5, 3)
8. Pour 4 quarts from the 5-quart conatiner into the 7-quart container. (4, 1, 7)
9. Empty the 7-quart container into the 12-quart container. (11, 1, 0)
10. Empty the 5-quart container into the 7-quart container. (11, 0, 1)
11. Fill the 5-quart container. (6, 5, 1)
12. Empty the 5-quart container into the 7-quart container. (6, 0, 6)

Teacher Pages: Science Problems (cont.)

Page 49: Taking the Temperature

With which temperature scale are the students most familiar? Point out that whether it is expressed as Fahrenheit or Celsius, the weather is the same. This is true of other measurements as well. In both math and science, exact labeling of numbers is critical. Because the Celsius scale is calibrated as a base 10 scale (decimal scale) it is often used in science. Encourage students to explore converting other measurement scales by first creating a measuring tool and then deriving a formula. The formula for converting Celsius to Fahrenheit is $F = 9/5\ C + 32$ or $(C° \times 1.8) + 32$. Gabriel Fahrenheit's scale may seem a bit arbitrary since it begins at 32. In creating his scale, Fahrenheit actually assigned 0 to the coldest temperature that he could achieve by adding salt to ice. Ask students to find the Celsius equivalent of this number. (-17.8° C)

Page 49 solution (chart): a. 40° C, hot; b. 86° F, warm; c. 20° C, mild; d. 50° F, cool.

Page 50: The Wind Beneath the Wings

Today we take air travel and even space exploration for granted, but it was not until 1903 that the Wright brothers and others finally achieved heavier-than-air-flight. The Bernoulli principle supplies an essential element in the design of aircraft. The forward movement, or thrust, provided by powerful engines forces air over the wings, creating lift. There are many applications of Bernoulli's principle as diverse as a spinning baseball and a sports car. Challenge the students to explain the role of lift in these areas. Have them create a miniwind tunnel using a small electric fan, or a blow dryer, and a clear plastic container. You may use a cardboard box by cutting a window and securely taping clear plastic over it to create a window. Stabilize the object to be tested. Adding smoke will make the air currents visible.

Page 51: Buoyant Boats

Why do some things float and others sink? Archimedes discovered that a liquid exerts a buoyant force on an object placed in it that is equal to the weight of the liquid that the object displaces. Archimedes' principle is applied to the design of boats, bridges, buoys, etc. This can be explored on its own in other physics experiments, and specific mathematical formulas can be applied to determine exact buoyancy, specific gravity, etc. When the students have built their boats, discuss which design allows the greatest weight to be placed on the foil. Try to elicit responses about surface area, weight distribution, etc. To expand this exploration, vary the material used for the boats, or repeat the experiment using another liquid like cooking oil or salt water. Compare the results with the results for water. Can the students reach any conclusion about the other liquids?

Page 52: Balancing Act

In this activity, students will explore science and math to create a piece of art. You may wish to extend the science application by discussing the many applications there are for simple machines, especially the inclined plane, or lever. Physics uses mathematics to determine the opposing forces and the efficiency of machines. Extend the activity by having students add one or more additional weights at the center of one or more arms of the mobile. Does this weight affect the balance of the arm? Ask them to explain why it does not.

Distances of The Planets from the Sun

Mapping the solar system is not an easy task. The distances are vast, and the planets, including Earth, are all moving. The orbital path of some planets is tilted. The table below shows the approximate distance of each planet from the Sun.

Planet	Distance	
	millions of miles	**millions of kilometers**
Mercury	36	58
Venus	67	108
Earth	93	150
Mars	142	228
Jupiter	486	778
Saturn	893	1,429
Uranus	1,797	2,875
Neptune	2,815	4,504
Pluto	3,688	5,900

If one (centimeter) inch = 1,000,000 miles, how large would a chart showing the distances need to be?

Determine a practical scale for such a chart, and create it on a separate piece of paper. Use the space below for your calculations.

Matter Matters

Matter is the basic building material of the universe. In its natural state, matter takes one of three forms: solid, liquid, and gas. By changing the conditions surrounding matter, it is possible to cause the matter to change from its normal state to another. For example, oxygen and nitrogen are gasses. When they are subjected to pressure, they become liquids.

Changes in the state of matter can most easily be observed in water. When the temperature of water is changed, it changes to a solid (ice) or a gas (steam). To demonstrate this, do the following experiment. Use the graph below to record your observations.

Measure an ice cube with a ruler. Use the measurements and the following formulas to determine the volume of the cube. An ice cube, for example, might measure 1.5 inches x 1 inch x 2 inches, or 3 cubic inches.

V = l x w x h (length x width x height)

Place the ice cube in a measured container. Use the markings on the container to measure and record the contents of the container. This is the liquid volume.

Use the following formulas to compare the solid volume of the cube to its liquid volume.

1 cubic inch = 1.8 fluid ounces   **1 cubic centimeter = 3.3 milliliters**

If the original mold for the ice cube is available, you may wish to pour the amount of liquid measured by your experiment into it. Does the liquid occupy as much space as the solid ice cube does? Do your calculations support your observations?

Use the grid below to create a graph that shows what happens to the liquid volume every 15 minutes. Use the liquid in the uncovered container.

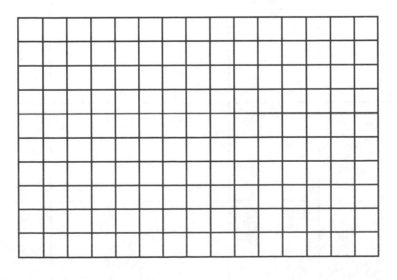

Challenge

Freeze identical cubes of olive oil, soda pop, coffee, milk, and juice. Place each in a measured container and follow the procedure above, using a different color to record the results for each liquid. Compare the condensation and evaporation rates.

Half Full

You have three containers. The first holds 12 quarts, the second holds seven quarts, and the last has a capacity of five quarts. If the first container is full and the others empty, can you divide the liquid into two portions?

One way to solve this puzzle is to graph each step. The X, or horizontal axis, represents the seven-quart container, while the vertical Y axis shows the five-quart container. The graph does not show the 12-quart container which is always in use. Any liquid not in the smaller containers is in the largest one.

Begin your graph at (0, 0) since both of the smaller containers are empty. Plot a point and draw a line to show each change in the contents of the containers.

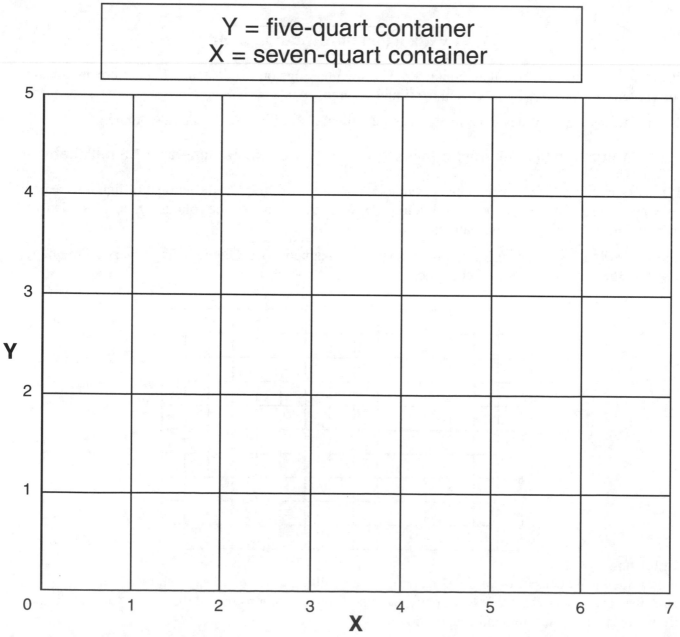

Y = five-quart container
X = seven-quart container

Taking the Temperature

Metric Mike always listens to the weather on radio station KMGO. His friend, Frank, relies on radio station WFAR. One day Frank was visiting Mike and happened to hear a weather forecast that predicted 20°. The next day Frank dressed for cold weather, but Mike wore only a light jacket. Who was dressed appropriately for the weather, and was it really cold or was it pleasant?

There are two scales used to give the temperature, the Fahrenheit thermometer and the Celsius, or centigrade, scale. Both measure exactly the same condition, but different numbers are used as labels.

When Gabriel Fahrenheit invented the mercury thermometer in 1714, he called the freezing point of water 32° and its boiling point 212°. This means that there are 180 integers between the two points. Later, Anders Celsius created a new temperature scale, using 0 to represent the freezing point of water and 100° for its boiling point. In this system, there are 100 integers between the two points.

Measure two strips of heavy paper to the length of two meter sticks or yardsticks. Label the end points of one strip 32 and 212. Mark and label the numbers between the two points at even intervals. Label the end points of the second strip as 0 and 100 and mark the intervals. By placing one strip below the other and aligning the freezing and boiling points, you can see both temperatures. Find the missing number for each pair below, and describe the weather for the day.

Celsius	Fahrenheit	Weather
	104°	
30°		
	68°	
10°		

Since it would be awkward to carry around two measuring strips, a formula or rule can be used to convert temperatures between the two scales.

To find the Celsius temperature, if the Fahrenheit temperature is given:

1. Subtract 32 from the Fahrenheit temperature. (F – 32)

2. Multiply by the ratio of points on the Fahrenheit scale to the points on the Celsius scale. (180/100 = 9/5 or 1.8)

3. The formula is C = (F – 32) x 1.8

Can you use the information above to find a formula to convert Celsius to Fahrenheit?

The Wind Beneath the Wings

For centuries, people yearned to fly. The air, it seemed, was the only aspect of the world that people could not dominate. They told legends and stories of those who mastered this feat and designed elaborate machines for flight, but no one was successful.

Daniel Bernoulli, a Swiss mathematician, finally found the key. He found that a rapidly moving fluid exerts less pressure than a slower moving fluid. Air is like a fluid. When air moves over the surface of a wing, its downward force is less than the upward force of the air beneath the object.
Try the following experiment:

1. Hold a long narrow strip of paper by one edge under your lips, so that the loose edge droops toward the floor.

2. Blow over the top of the paper.

The paper will rise because the air on the top is moving faster and exerting less pressure, while the air at the bottom continues to push up against the paper.

Bird wings and airplane wings curve more on the top than on the bottom, which makes the air speed up as it passes over the top of the wing. This shape is called an airfoil. The pressure of the air below the wing provides about 15 percent of the force needed to lift an airplane. The suction caused by the faster moving air at the top of the wing pulling away supplies the remaining force needed to lift the airplane. Shape, area, and tilt of the wing determine its effectiveness and the amount of lift it can provide.

Create the Best Wing Shapes

Design several different wing shapes from stiff paper, varying the size and curvature. To determine how effective each one is, build a wind tunnel. Cut a large window in one side of a 10" x 10" x 20" (25 cm x 25 cm x 50 cm) box, leaving a 1-inch (2.54 cm) frame. Tape clear plastic sheeting over the window. Cut large windows in the ends of the box. Secure a small dowel to the bottom of the box with modeling clay. Attach threads to the edges of the wing to be tested, and mount the wing on top of the dowel. Position a small electric fan so that it faces the wing. Observe the airflow. Record what happens by making a sketch on the back of this page. Use your results to determine the best design.

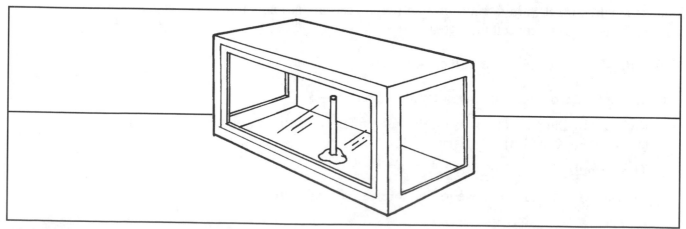

Buoyant Boats

What makes an object or a person float or sink in a liquid? The answer lies in the upward force, or buoyant force, of the liquid against the object. If the upward force is greater than the weight of the object, the object will float. Use this information to design a foil boat that will hold as many pennies as possible without sinking,

To build the boat, you will need the following materials: one 3" by 5" (8 cm x 13 cm) piece of aluminum foil, a pan of water, and several pennies.

Float the piece of aluminum foil on the surface of the water. The force of the water pushing up allows the foil to float. Now begin placing pennies on the foil. Continue until the foil begins to sink. In the first box of the chart below, sketch the pattern of the pennies and record the number of pennies you were able to place on the foil.

Design 1	Design 2
number of pennies _____	number of pennies _____
Design 3	Design 4
number of pennies _____	number of pennies _____

Next, fold the foil to create a boat shape. Float your boat and add as many pennies as you can. See how many pennies you can put in your boat before it sinks. Sketch your design in Design 2 box and record the number of pennies you placed in it.

Repeat the experiment two more times, changing the design of your boat for each trial and recording the results. The only thing you can change is the design; you cannot change the materials.

Based on your chart and those of your classmates, which design was the most successful? Can you explain why? Write your conclusion here: _____

_____

_____

_____

Balancing Act

Levers are simple machines that can be used to make work easier. Another application of the lever is a seesaw. When the weights on the ends of the seesaw are unequal, the heavier weight must be moved closer to the center to achieve balance. Similarly, a lightweight stick suspended by a thread tied to its center will rotate if unequal weights are suspended from the ends. The tendency to rotate in one direction or another is called torque, and it can be found mathematically. The amount of torque is equal to the weight times the distance between the weight and the axis about which the stick can rotate. Do the following activity to learn about the ratio of weight to distance, and use what you discover to create a mobile.

Materials: small-diameter wood dowels or bamboo garden stakes (2 feet/.6 meters), supply of identical weights (heavy washers, fishing sinkers, bolts), string, scissors

Directions

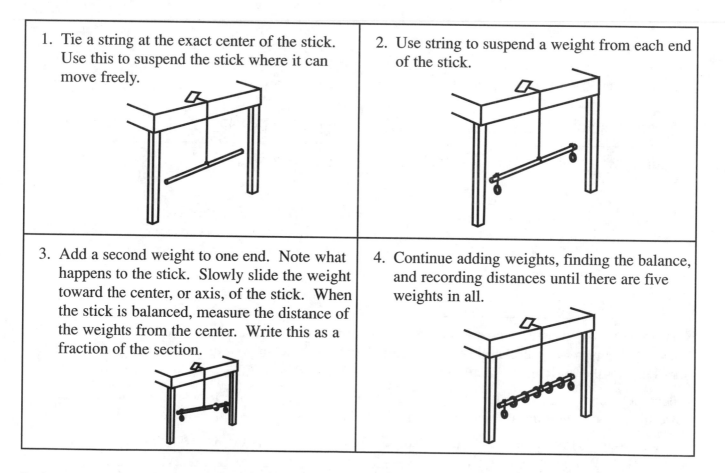

1. Tie a string at the exact center of the stick. Use this to suspend the stick where it can move freely.

2. Use string to suspend a weight from each end of the stick.

3. Add a second weight to one end. Note what happens to the stick. Slowly slide the weight toward the center, or axis, of the stick. When the stick is balanced, measure the distance of the weights from the center. Write this as a fraction of the section.

4. Continue adding weights, finding the balance, and recording distances until there are five weights in all.

Is there a correlation between the number of weights and the fractions you recorded? Explain your answer on the back of this paper.

Now Try This

Draw a design for a mobile with five arms. Use the information you gathered above to plan the placement of the weights and rods. Gather materials based on your design and build a mobile.

Teacher Pages: Art Problems

Page 55: Origami Geometry

Origami is the Japanese art of folding paper to create flowers, animals, and many other objects. Many mathematical concepts can be proved or demonstrated using paperfolding. Challenge the students to find other theorems that can be shown by folding paper. Vary the initial shape if necessary.

Page 56: Tessellations

If you can find some Escher prints to show the students, it will help them see art in another way. The word tessellation comes from Latin and originally referred to small pieces used to form a mosaic. Tessellations can be observed in ceramic tiles and in Eastern art. After the students do a simple tessellation, challenge them to create a more complicated one. Have them collect examples of tessellations they observe and share them with the class. Display the students' tessellations in the classroom.

Page 57: The Golden Section

This concept, also called the divine proportion, golden ratio or golden proportion, is closely related to Fibonacci numbers. It can be seen in the Egyptian pyramids, the Parthenon, and the United Nations building. Renaissance artists applied the golden ratio to depict an ideal human figure, to determine the best dimensions for a painting, and to place figures within a scene. Many people perceive art and even geometric figures as more aesthetically pleasing when the golden section is employed. In a golden rectangle, the sides are in the same relation as the golden section. If a square with sides equal to the width of the golden rectangle is cut from a golden rectangle, the result is another golden rectangle. (See diagram.) Because phi, the golden ratio, is close to the ratio between Fibonnaci numbers, use numbers from that sequence to create lines and rectangles. Can the students create a golden triangle?

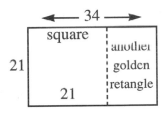

Page 58: Cuboctahedron-Truncum

Is it possible to represent a three-dimensional figure on a single plane? Albrecht Dürer did just that to show the relationship of all the faces of a complex figure. In this exercise, the students must take familiar solid shapes and draw them in one dimension, showing how the pieces fit together.

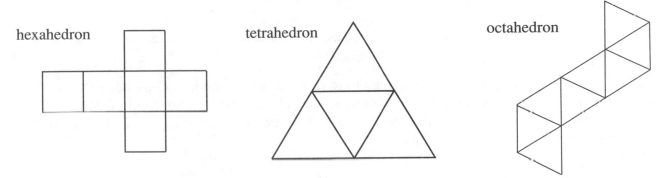

hexahedron

tetrahedron

octahedron

Teacher Pages: Art Problems (cont.)

Page 59: Gaining Perspective

This activity provides some simple guidelines for creating the illusion of three dimensions on a single plane. To introduce this topic, display paintings in the classroom that show the use of perspective, as well as some that do not. Engage the students in a discussion about the subject matter and the presentation in these paintings.

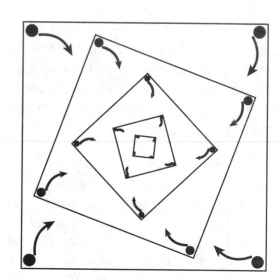

Page 60: Straight-Line Spirals

If the spirals are drawn neatly with a sharp pencil, you will see all sorts of interesting things. Students may at first be confused about the direction of the spiders. Stress to them that the spider's right is not the viewer's right. Let the students explore a variety of shapes. For example, what happens when you create nested triangles? Make a classroom art display of such ideas.

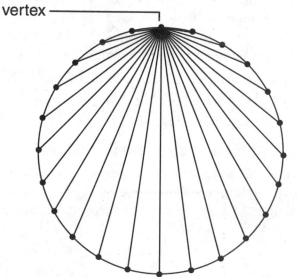

vertex

Page 61: Embroidery

You may be able to find someone who does intricate embroidery to demonstrate to the class. See if anyone in your class knows of anyone who embroiders. A hobby shop owner might know of someone who would be willing to show students what they have created with string.

Sample of a set of diagonals from one vertex (22 diagonals)

Page 62: Mirror Imaging

The familiar commutative law does not always apply to flips and spins of objects. Symmetry can be described in terms of the number of turns and rotations that can be made without changing the appearance of the object. A sphere has the greatest possible symmetry. Challenge students to apply the principles of symmetry to a number of objects.

Origami Geometry

Some people think that the only way you can prove or demonstrate geometric theorems is to do a lengthy word proof. This is not always true. Using actual models often makes ideas and concepts easier to understand. Many concepts can be proved or demonstrated using paperfolding. The following is one way to show that the angles of a triangle are equal to 180 degrees.

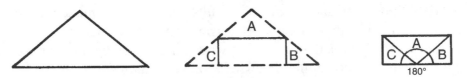

Follow the directions below. Note the importance of understanding the geometric terms.

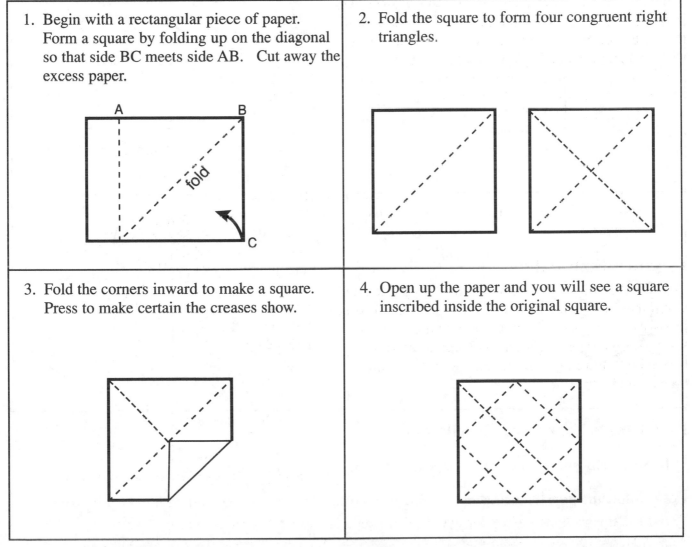

1. Begin with a rectangular piece of paper. Form a square by folding up on the diagonal so that side BC meets side AB. Cut away the excess paper.

2. Fold the square to form four congruent right triangles.

3. Fold the corners inward to make a square. Press to make certain the creases show.

4. Open up the paper and you will see a square inscribed inside the original square.

Note that the inscribed square is one half the area of the large square. This is one geometry-related characteristic of the paperfolding activity described above. Work with paper to see if you can demonstrate one or more geometric theorems you discovered as a result of your paperfolding.

Tessellations

A tessellation is a design that covers a plane. The design does not overlap and there are no gaps in it. Maurice C. Escher, a Dutch artist, was fascinated with tessellations. In many of his sketches he used various forms of tessellations. If you can find prints of his works, look at them carefully. You will see how he rotated and transformed tessellations to create many of his sketches.

The word *tessera* comes from Latin and means the small squares used to make a mosaic. In a tessellation, a pattern is formed from a single shape. The shape is modified in some way and repeated to fill the available space. Many tessellations are very complicated and contain non-geometric figures. The following are directions for one geometric tessellation you can make.

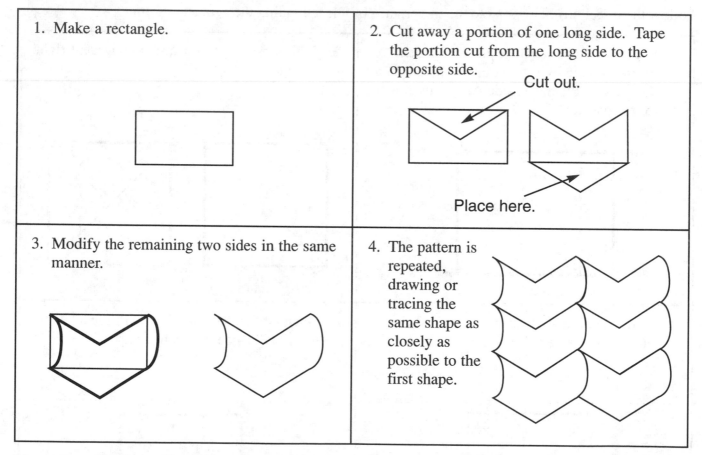

1. Make a rectangle.

2. Cut away a portion of one long side. Tape the portion cut from the long side to the opposite side.

   Cut out.

   Place here.

3. Modify the remaining two sides in the same manner.

4. The pattern is repeated, drawing or tracing the same shape as closely as possible to the first shape.

Now Create Your Own Tessellation

1. Select any simple geometric shape and draw it on a separate piece of paper.

2. Follow the process used above, removing a portion from a side and adding it to an adjacent or opposite side.

3. When you are satisfied with the shape you have created, trace it on a piece of heavy paper like posterboard or cardstock and cut it out. Use this as a template and fill a page with your design.

When you have filled the page, add shadings and/or color to make your picture more interesting.

The Golden Section

A line segment may be divided into two sections an infinite number of ways. Some people believe that there is one division of the line that is more beautiful than any other. The ancient Greeks called this division the golden section. It has also been called the golden mean, the golden ratio, and the divine proportion. What makes this division unique? The answer lies in the proportion of parts and the whole. A line is divided into a golden section when the ratio of the length of the whole to the larger part equals the ratio of the larger part to the smaller part.

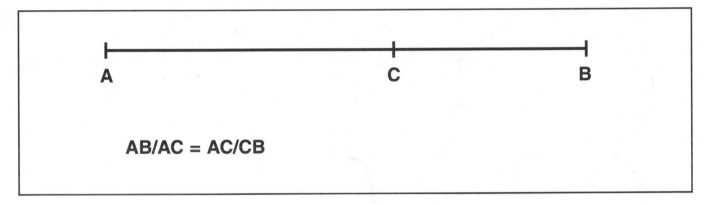

AB/AC = AC/CB

If the ratio of AC/CB is 1.618033988, the line is a golden section. The Greeks called this number phi.

phi = 1.618033988 (the ratio of AC/CB)

This is also the ratio of consecutive numbers in the Fibonacci sequence!

There are many applied examples of this proportion in art and architecture. In mathematics, a rectangle is called a golden rectangle if its sides are in this proportion with a length of AB and a width of AC. A golden triangle is a right isosceles triangle with sides the length of AB and a base length of CB.

In the space below, construct a large golden rectangle. Draw a line to divide the rectangle into a square and a smaller rectangle. Find the ratio of the sides of the newly formed rectangle. Is it a golden rectangle? If so, can you make more golden rectangles within it?

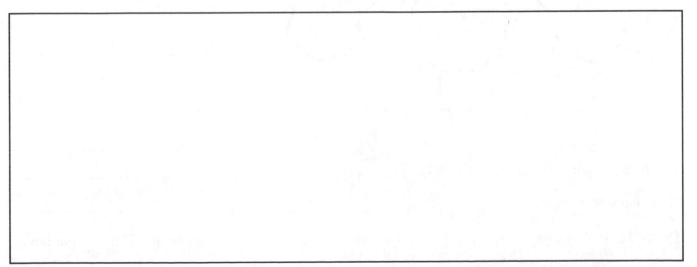

Cuboctahedron-Truncum

Albrecht Dürer (1471–1528) was one of eighteen children in his family. Dürer's father, a goldsmith, hoped that his son would follow his profession. He apprenticed the boy to an artist to learn engraving and painting. Dürer felt that mathematics, especially geometry, enhanced art, and he wrote books on mathematics.

One of the things Dürer did was to describe or draw solids which are three-dimensional on a plane in their unassembled form. Here is a cuboctahedron-truncum.

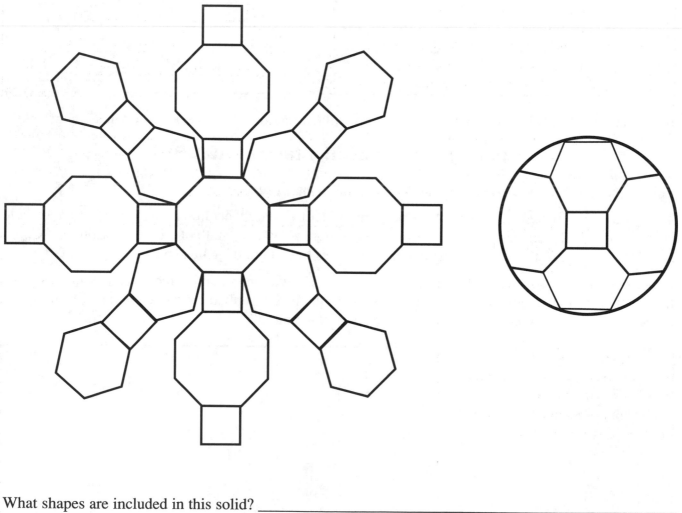

What shapes are included in this solid? _____

How many of each are there? _____

On the back of this page, draw a cube (hexahedron), tetrahedron, and octahedron as Dürer might have.

Gaining Perspective

A canvas or piece of paper has only two dimensions—height and width. A picture with only two dimensions looks flat. Artists use mathematics to create pictures that show a third dimension—depth.

When you look at things in the distance, there is a point at which the sky seems to touch the earth. This is called the horizon line. The artist decides where the horizon line, or eye level of the viewer, will be for the picture.

The artist then decides on a vanishing point. This is located on the horizon line and is the central point of the picture. Parallel lines drawn from this point to the edges of the paper or canvas help the artist place figures and objects in the picture.

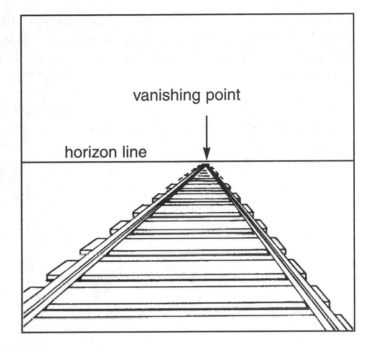

A good way to visualize the vanishing point is to think about railroad tracks. You know that the sides of the tracks are parallel, but if you look at a long straight set of tracks, they seem to come closer together the farther away they are. This is the same kind of illusion that the artist uses. The closer an object is to the vanishing point, the smaller and more indistinct it becomes.

Try this experiment. Draw a square in the box on the right. Now add lines to turn it into a cube. Can you see how parallel lines added a dimension to the square?

On a separate piece of paper, design a masterpiece. Begin by lightly marking the horizon line, vanishing point, and rays. Use these as a guide to create a landscape scene.

Straight Line Spirals

Spirals are mathematical shapes that look like they are moving. Antlers of goats, insides of flowers, seashells, DNA structure, and plant growths have spiral formations.

This is an example of a spiral created from a nest of squares.

Straight line spirals are formed by making a nest of regular polygons in which each smaller polygon is formed by connecting the midpoints of the sides of the larger polygon.

Find the spiral in this drawing.

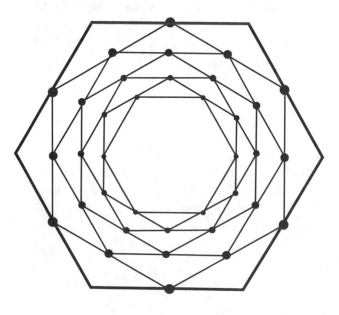

Challenge

Four spiders start crawling from the four corners of a square. Each spider is crawling in a clockwise direction, moving toward the center at a constant rate. Every spider is always located at the corner of a square. Draw the nest of squares and, using a different colored pencil for each spider, trace its path. Where are the spirals?

Embroidery

Curves can be formed with straight line segments. Some people create this pattern with thread, using the art of embroidery. Follow the directions below to create curves by drawing only straight line segments.

Begin by making a 24-sided polygon out of the circle below. One of the ways you can do this is by marking the circle like a clock. This will give you 12 vertices. Next make another mark in the space each hour. You now have 24 marks on the circle. Connect the marks to make a 24-sided polygon. Carefully draw in all the possible diagonals from each vertex. Use a sharp pencil and make your lines as thin as possible. If you do this correctly you will see a series of concentric circles.

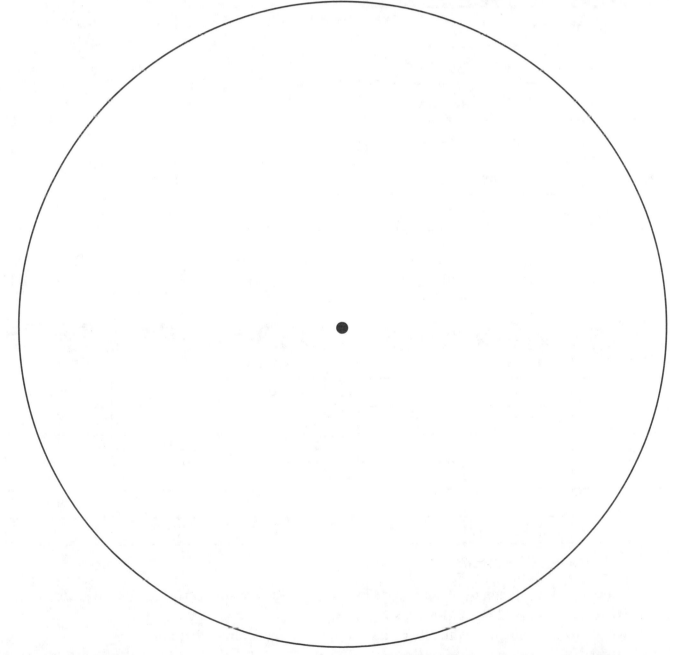

Mirror Imaging

How many different ways can you flip and rotate an object and leave it in a position that appears to be the same as the original? The answer will depend on the shape of the object, but the greater the number of such operations, the more symmetrical the object is. A sphere has the maximum symmetry possible.

The diagram and table below show several possible ways to flip or rotate an object. There are three rotations and two flip, in addition to the possibility that nothing is done to the object.

Table of Operations	
0	do nothing
1	rotate 90° counter clockwise
2	rotate 180° counter clockwise
3	rotate 270° counter clockwise
4	flip over D–D axis
5	flip over E–E axis

E

D ———————————— D

E

Activities

1. Make cardboard cutouts of four alphabet letters. Perform six operations on each letter and record the results on a chart similar to the ones below.

The Letter J		
Operation	Result	Change?
0	J	No
1	⌐	Yes
2	⌐	Yes
3	⌐	Yes
4	⌐	Yes
5	⌐	Yes

Square ■		
Operation	Result	Change?
0	☐	No
1	☐	No
2	☐	No
3	☐	No
4	☐	No
5	☐	No

Which is more symmetrical?

2. Try rotating and flipping different objects like flowers, snowflakes, starfish shapes, regular polygons, etc. Record and analyze the results.

3. Make a chart and diagram with other flips and rotations of several other objects.

Teacher Pages: Music Problems

Music is extremely mathematical. Pitch (frequency) and volume (amplitude) are musical terms which translate to numbers. Music translates to higher mathematics with exponential functions. If your students want to look at this, have them graph y = 2x. This will give them a curve that fits the curve of sounds. Use this opportunity to expose the students to modern classical music, which has some definite new sounds. Challenge the students to apply what they learn about the mathematics and theory of music to their own favorite styles and performers. Invite dialogue and the exchange of ideas.

Many of the concepts associated with music are not confined to music. Patterns of meter and rhythm apply to poetry and literature as well. Encourage students to develop a sense of rhythm by listening to a variety of music. Understanding and recognizing the beat adds to the students' appreciation of all kinds of music. In more sophisticated music, the emphasis may change, creating syncopations in the beat. This is especially true of Latin music and jazz. See if the students can pick up on that. Ask them how they respond to simple and more complex rhythms. Which music makes them want to tap their feet, snap their fingers or clap their hands? Look for the rhythmic patterns that occur naturally, like heartbeats and falling rain.

Page 65: Sound Ideas

If you have a piano in the school, it might be fun to look inside the piano. Concert or grand pianos have the shape that we are discussing here. Open the piano and show students the variations in the dimensions of the strings and how they are arranged. Point out the felt tip on each "hammer," as well as the sounding board. Compare the piano to other stringed instruments. If any of your students play, have them give a concert for the rest of the class. If not, invite someone in to play for the students.
Note: The frequencies given are those used in physics. Tuning forks used in laboratories have a frequency of 256 cycles per second for middle C. When C is 256 cycles per second, A above middle C is 427 cycles per second. However, the American Federation of Music has adopted 440 cycles/sec for A above middle C, and the scales used by musicians are based on this standard. If a C tuning fork is available, you may want to compare it to the piano.
Solutions: C, 1; D, 9/8; E, 5/4; F, 4/3; G, 3/2; A, 5/3; B, 15/8; C, 2; D, 576; E, 640; F, 683

Page 66: Eight Is Not Enough

The previous activity focused on the pitch or frequency for the eight notes of the diatonic scale. Adding five half tones changes the scale to a chromatic scale. Ask students to consider which scale is more versatile. Here it might be interesting to note that there is a mathematical difference between many of the half tones. C sharp has a frequency of 266 cycles per second and D flat has a frequency of 276 cycles per second. If all the possible scales were built, an octave would have about 70 keys. The compromise is called a tempered scale, and it is based on even intervals for the 12 notes of the octave.

Remind the students that a square root is a number that can be multiplied by itself to produce a number. Discuss other exponents and show that roots can be found for any exponent. For example, $3^3 = 27$ and $\sqrt[3]{27} = 3$. In this problem, the ratio must be a number that equals 2 when multiplied by itself 12 times, or the twelfth root of 2. That number is calculated as 1.05946.

Teacher Pages: Music Problems (cont.)

Page 66: Eight Is Not Enough (cont.)

	C	D	E	F	G	A	B	C	D	E	F	G	A	B
Key of C	256	288	320	341	384	426	480	512						
Key of D		288	324	**360**	384	432	480	**540**	576					
Key of E			320	**360**	**400**	427	480	**533**	600	640				
Key of F				341	383	426	**455**	512	568	639	682			
Key of G					384	432	480	512	576	665	**710**	768		
Key of A						426	480	**532**	568	639	**710**	799	852	
Key of B							480	**540**	**600**	640	**720**	800	900	960

Page 67: Reading Music

Many students learn to sing by listening to music and do not know how to read music. The treble clef and key signature may seem like Greek to them. If you have students who know how to read music, you might ask them to teach the class how to do this. It is extremely logical and mathematical. Transposing music will demonstrate that the relationship or interval between the notes does not change, although the pitch does. The activity can be done on paper, or on a keyboard instrument. If students wish to explore further, have them try writing the same song in other keys.

Page 68: Musical Time

This activity builds on the previous one and gives students key information about music composition. If a piano is available, play some of their rhythms. For this purpose, all the notes can be the same. Students may also clap in rhythm or tap beats with a pencil on a desk.

Page 69: A Minute Waltz

The first note of a measure of music is called the downbeat and is usually stressed. Often a composer will follow the rule for several measures and then change to a new pattern, emphasizing a previously unstressed beat. In some cases the timing changes slightly as well, substituting a multiple or a subdivision of the beat. Drums are often used to provide the rhythm.

Once students can identify the downbeat, the first note of a measure of music, they should be able to identify the time signature of the piece. There are some recordings available that contain only the rhythms of various kinds of music. Tempo, or the speed at which a piece is played, can vary greatly from one conductor or band leader to another. All waltzes are written in three-quarter time with three beats to a measure and one beat to each quarter note, but there is a distinct difference between the tempo of a Strauss or Viennese waltz which has about 54 measures per minute and a slow waltz, played at about 30 measures per minute.

Sound Ideas

Sound is all around us. Vibrating matter produces a wave-like disturbance which is transmitted, usually through air, to a receiver like the human ear. Sounds can be pleasant or unpleasant, depending on a number of factors. Music is sound produced by matter which vibrates in a regular fashion.

In a piano, sound is produced by strings. Pushing the key of a piano causes a hammer to hit a string and produce a sound. Because the strings are of different lengths and diameters, each string vibrates at a different rate, creating a different sound or note. The shorter a string is, the more rapidly it vibrates, and the more rapid the vibration, the higher the sound. If the length of a string is cut in half, the speed at which it vibrates, called the frequency, doubles. In music, the interval between tones that have this half ratio is called an octave. The word octave means eight, and there are eight steps or notes between the two tones.

The frequency of middle C on a piano is 256 cycles per second, and the frequency of high C is 512. Below are the frequencies for the notes of an octave. Write a fraction to show the ratio between middle C and each note.

Note	Frequency	Fraction
middle C	256	
D	288	
E	320	
F	341	
G	384	
A	426	
B	480	
high C	512	

Use eight identical glass bottles, or eight test tubes, to create a scale. Add water to each one. Tune the glasses so that each one is one full tone higher than the previous one. Measure the height of the water for each note. Use ratios to compare the notes. Is there some similarity? Explain your findings.

_____

_____

_____

Eight Is Not Enough

Suppose the scale began at D instead of at C. Use the ratios from the previous exercise (shown below) to determine the frequency for each note of the new scale. Write them in the chart.

Key of	C	D	E	F	G	A	B	C	D	E	F	G	A	B
C	256	288	320	341	384	426	480	512						
D		288						576						
E			320											
F				341										
G					384									
A						426								
B							480							
C								512						

Challenge

Some of the notes in each new scale have the same cycles per second as the C scale. Circle those that are not the same and find the new ratios. These notes are created by the black keys on the piano. If they raise the tone, they are called sharps. If they lower the tone, they are called flats. There are five half tones in each octave. A scale that has twelve tones is called a chromatic scale.

If all the variations in cycles per second in the scales above were represented on a keyboard, each octave would have 70 keys. Can you think of a way to assign frequencies to the twelve notes of the chromatic scale so that the intervals are even?

_____

_____

_____

_____

_____

Reading Music

To play a particular piece of music on a musical instrument or sing a song, the sequence of individual tones or notes can be written down. Music is written by using symbols for notes on a staff, which is like a graph. The musical staff has five lines and four spaces, each with an assigned note of the scale. The lines represent E, G, B, D, and F, while the spaces are F, A, C, and E. In order to accommodate the eight notes of the octave that begins with middle C, D is written directly below the last line of the staff, and a line is added below the staff for C.

Other important information is given at the beginning of the staff. On an instrument like the piano, notes may be played by both hands, so there are two staffs, one for the higher notes played by the right hand and one for the lower notes played by the left hand. Most instruments and singers use only one staff. The symbol at the beginning indicates whether the notes are to be played in the higher, or treble clef, or the lower bass clef. On the staff for the bass clef, middle C is on a line above the staff.

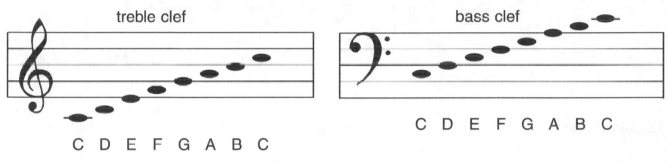

One or more sharp ♯ or flat ♭ symbols on the lines or spaces of the staff indicate the key in which a piece is to be played. Sometimes a singer or musician wants to perform a piece in a key different from the one in which the piece was written. Because of the mathematical relationship, any piece can be transposed, or changed, to another key. See if you can rewrite the notes below. The melody should sound the same, but the pitch will vary. Check your work by playing the original and your transposition on a piano. Do they sound the same?

Musical Time

One other very important piece of information included on the staff of any piece of music is called the time signature. This tells the person reading it how long to hold each note and where stress should be placed. This information looks like a fraction. The top number tells how many beats there are in a measure of music. The measures are indicated by vertical lines drawn through the staff. In most written music there are 3, 4, or 6 beats to a measure.

The shape of each note on the staff indicates its value. A whole note has a value of one. There are also half, quarter, eighth, sixteenth, thirty-second, and sixty-fourth notes.

The bottom number in the time signature indicates which kind of note receives one beat. The most common key signature uses four, meaning that a quarter note receives one beat.

On the musical staffs below, see how many different combinations of notes you can make to complete one measure. Note that usually this rhythm is consistent throughout a piece of music.

A Minute Waltz

The time signature is an essential part of written music. The time signature tells us how long to hold each note in relation to the other notes in the same measure or piece of music, but it does not give an exact time. Sometimes phrases are written on the piece of music to indicate how loud or soft and how slowly or quickly a particular piece should be played.

In a concert, the conductor is responsible for setting the tempo (speed). He or she uses a baton or his or her hand to set the tempo. The musicians watch for signals that indicate the downbeat, or first note, of the measure. Serious students of music may use a metronome to establish tempo for their playing.

Listen to several different pieces of music. Include a Strauss waltz like "The Blue Danube," a contemporary waltz like "Moon River," a fast rock and roll song, and a ballad.

Record the name of the music on the chart below.

Listen to several measures and identify the downbeat. Count the beats from one downbeat to the next to find the beats per measure.

Record the time signature.

Use a watch with a minute hand or a stopwatch to time yourself and begin counting the number of measures in a minute. Be as precise as you can.

Record the number of measures per minute and calculate how many beats per minute the song has.

Title	Time Signature	Measures per Minute	Beats per Minute

Teacher Pages: Money Problems

The most used and often practical application of mathematics is dealing with currency. Students are often unaware of the economic facts of life and ill prepared to deal with real-life situations.

Page 72: The Good Life

Many students take part-time jobs while they are in school to help pay their expenses or to earn money for something they want to own. Most young people begin working for minimum wage, an amount set by the state and federal governments. Many are surprised to learn that their net pay is not the same as their hourly wage. This exercise is designed to provide the students with a different perspective on the value of items they might buy. It provides an alternative method of determining the cost of an item and may lead to a better understanding of what money really represents. This activity may easily be expanded to include buying larger items, like a car. You may also wish to explore median incomes with home prices, etc., determining the average hours of work at the average wage to purchase the average home.

Page 73: An Ancient Problem

This exercise is a good introduction to the use of exponents. Most mathematicians do not like to do tedious calculations like repetitive multiplication or long division. Explain that exponents are a fast way to multiply, and are a kind of mathematical shorthand. Demonstrate that adding one to the exponent doubles the base number: $2^1 = 2$, $2^2 = 4$, $2^3 = 8$, etc. In this problem, all squares after the first are doubled, or squared. The amount of money received by doubling pennies for every square can be found by raising two to the power of the number of squares in which the amount doubles (2^{63}) and adding the amount from the first square (.01): $2^{63} + .01 = \$ 92,\ 233,720,\ 368,\ 547,\ 800.\ 01$. Demonstrate using a calculator to solve this problem. This number is usually displayed as scientific notation.

Page 74: Counting the Old-Fashioned Way

The abacus uses base 10, which means that it is very similar to counting on our fingers. Demonstrate to the students how you could count with only seven fingers. Begin counting. When you reach five, put up one finger on the other hand to represent five. The first hand is back to zero. This is the process used to count on an abacus. If you are lucky enough to find someone who knows how to use an abacus quickly, invite him or her to demonstrate for the class how quickly calculation can be done on an abacus. Ask the person to share with the class how he or she learned arithmetic.

Page 75: Choices

These are real problems that have answers that are based on a variety of factors other than pure mathematics. For example, a question to ask about the first problem might be, "How often do you want to eat tacos on Thursday night, and how many tacos will you buy each Thursday?" Use simple math to calculate how many tacos you must buy at the discount price to pay for the shirt ($12.99/.25 = 52$). For the problem with the $25 per month versus 10 cents a mile, you might ask students to think about their own distance from school and possible scenarios. Create other real-life situations to help students with their money problem-solving skills, and encourage the students to find other examples of such decisions. They are fun to research and work out.

Teacher Pages: Money Problems (cont.)

Page 76: Taking a Loan
Students do not really understand money until they have to deal with it. Many times students do not learn this until they get into trouble with credit cards. Get students to see that there are many ways to save and borrow money. Having a banker come in and explain this might be interesting. Stocks and bonds might be a subject some students might like to learn about. When it comes to money, some students are always fascinated.

Page 77: Money Makes Money
Students need to learn about the choices that are available for saving money as well as spending it. Stress factors like length of time for the investment, rate, etc., that can affect decisions on where and how to invest. If you have time, have the students study the stock market. Tell each student that he or she has $1000 to invest in stocks. They must research the companies, make an investment, and track their stock selections for a period of time. Is stock market investing a sure thing?

Page 78: The Cookie Business
This exercise involves the steps to create a business plan. Having a great idea or a wonderful product is not enough. This activity may inspire entrepreneurial activities. Even if the business never gets past the paper stage, students will benefit from the process. Remind them that many millionaires have failed in business more than once. They reached the top because they did not quit and learned from their failures.

Page 79: Buying a Car
The purpose of the exercise is to show students that saving for a car (or any major purchase) is better than entering into a loan situation in which they will end up paying for the car two or three times. Buying on credit is very compelling. You can have what you want now rather than later. This is a good time to show students how advertising appeals to our need to have something now.

Page 80: The Pyramid Scheme
This is a very simplified version of the pyramid. In actual practice, the individuals at any level can recruit more than two people. The actual percentage may be a great deal less than the 25 pecent in the example, but the net may be more because it is coming from a vast number of people. The scheme is often tied to the sale of a product or service. To show graphically how the "pyramid scheme," also known as multi-level marketing or MLM, hurts the people on the bottom, enact the scenario with play money.

Answers:
1. No. The person at the top received more than the others.
2. Two more levels must be added before the person on Level 3 makes back the amount he or she invested.
3. The people on Level 5 receive $50.00 per person recruited, or $100 each. On Level 4, each individual receives $150.00 ($37.50 for each person on Level 6). Each individual at Level 3 takes $28.125 for each new recruit, or a total of $225. The people at Level 2 keep $21.09375 of each new investment, or $337.50 each. The person at Level 1 makes a total of $2,025: $63.28125 for each of the 32 individuals recruited for Level 6.

The Good Life

You have taken a part-time job at a local fast food restaurant. They will pay you a minimum wage of $5.00 per hour. Because you are still going to school, you can work a maximum of 20 hours a week. When you are paid, you plan to spend some of your money and save the rest. Although you are being paid $5.00 per hour, taxes and Social Security amounting to 15 percent are deducted from your paycheck. What is your net pay per hour?

On payday, you and your friends decide to go to the movies. Your ticket costs $7.50, and popcorn is $2.50. After the show you spend $2.75 for a soda and fries. The evening costs a total of $12.75. If you divide the total cost by your net hourly wage, you will see that you worked three hours to pay for the evening.

Do some research to find out what the current minimum wage is in your area and what the average deductions are. Determine the net pay per hour. Enter your answers in the chart below.

Find out the current price of three items you would like to purchase with your earnings. Some examples are clothing, tapes or CDs, a video game, or special sports or hobby supplies.

Write the name of the item and its cost in the chart. Calculate the number of hours you will have to work to earn each item.

minimum wage	_____
deductions	_____
net wages	_____

Item	cost in $	cost in hours

An Ancient Problem

There once was a king who had a great kingdom and great riches. The king discovered a young scholar who showed great promise. He offered the young scholar half of his kingdom or one grain of wheat on a chessboard doubled for every square. What do you suppose the young scholar chose?

Make this ancient problem more meaningful to you by solving the following problem: Someone has offered you a million dollars or one penny doubled for every square of a checkerboard. The board is drawn below. Use the checkerboard and some paper to calculate which is the better choice.

Write your decision here: _____

_____

_____

_____

Counting the Old-Fashioned Way

The Chinese abacus is a forerunner to our modern calculators and computers. It has rods with five beads below and two beads above a crossbar within a wooden or plastic frame. The diagrams below show how the beads of an abacus are manipulated to solve problems. Each column of beads is like the "places" in our number system. The lower, or earth beads are each worth 1 and the upper, or heaven beads are each worth 5. Begin with all the beads moved away from the divider—heaven beads up and earth beads down. Choose any column to work with as the "ones" place. To show a number such as 3, simply move three earth beads up. To show the number 7, move one heaven bead down and two earth beads up.

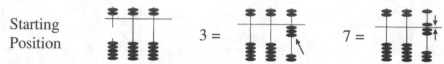

How would you represent the number 30? If you moved three earth beads up in the next column to the left, you are absolutely right. Which column would you use to show 300? Read the numbers on the picture abacuses below. Then draw diagrams to show the following numbers on an abacus: 33, 77, 4, 146, 908, and 21.

Now try to solve simple arithmetic problems. Use the following addition and subtraction problem samples:

Addition: To add 25 + 12, place 25 on the abacus. Without clearing the beads, move 12 more as shown. Look at the resulting number. Does it show 37?

Note: If at any time both heaven beads in a column are used up, carry 1 earth bead up in the next column to take their places and clear the two heaven beads back away. For example, 7 + 5 would change like this:

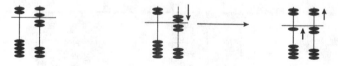

Subtraction: To subtract 44–13, simply take away the second number of beads (13).

Try a variety of addition and subtraction problems.
Note: Sometimes you may have to regroup (borrow) from a higher column by exchanging a higher earth bead for two lower heaven beads to be able to complete the subtraction.

Choices

In a previous exercise we saw how we made decisions based on value. The following exercises are taken from real-life examples. The answer to each is found in how often you intend to buy or use the product or service. Answer the question by showing your work on each.

A Mexican restaurant sells tacos for $1.50. As part of their special "Taco Thursday" promotion, if you wear a T-shirt printed with the restaurant logo that advertises "Taco Thursday," you can buy the tacos for $1.25 each. The shirt costs $12.99. Should you buy a shirt? Will you really save money on the tacos? What other factors are there?

_____

_____

_____

Your friend's mother has a car and is willing to drive you to school for $25 a month or 10 cents a mile. Suppose you live 2.7 miles from the school. Calculate which deal you should take. Consider your other options.

_____

_____

_____

_____

_____

There is a bookstore that buys and sells paperback books. This is how it works. If your paperback book is in good shape and they do not have too many of those books, they will give you 25 percent of its cover price. The price to buy a used book is 50 percent of the cover price plus a $ .15 carrying charge. Suppose you were able to collect 50 paperbacks from your relatives and neighbors. You take the books to the store and are given a credit. Do some research and see how much they would be worth. How many books could you "purchase" before you have to sell other books or pay money?

_____

_____

_____

_____

_____

Taking a Loan

Sometimes people need to borrow money for a large purchase, like a house, a car, or to pay for an education. Banks allow people to borrow money for a fee, or interest. The bank is in the business of making money, and it must cover its operating expenses and give a share of the interest it earns from loans to those who have deposited money in savings programs. So the interest charged for a loan will be more than the interest they pay for a savings account. The bank also will try to make certain that they will get the money back. The bank may require someone trustworthy to guarantee the loan, or they may ask for collateral, something of value that the person owns, that can be taken and sold if the loan is not paid.

The cost of the loan will be computed for a given period of time, and the borrower will have to make monthly payments which include a portion of the principle, or amount borrowed, and the interest.

Research current interest rates and calculate the true cost of borrowing $100 for one year.

Credit cards offer another way to borrow money. Generally the interest charged by a credit card company is higher than that charged by the bank. Credit card companies do not require collateral, so all customers must pay more to make up for those who do not pay.

Research at least two major credit cards. Determine the cost to borrow $100 for one year. Remember to include any annual fee the credit card company may charge for their card.

Decide on an item you would like to buy. Research the best buy for this item. Use the information you gathered to fill in the chart below indicating a possible way to finance each of your purchases. Analyze the data and decide whether you will save for the item, borrow from the bank, or use a credit card.

	Type		
	Savings	**Bank**	**Credit Card**
Cost of item			
Time to get money			
When I can get item			
How much will it cost me			

My analysis: _____

_____

_____

_____

Money Makes Money

Imagine that you have just received a gift of $100 and have decided that instead of spending it, you will save it for a big expense or purchase in the future, like a car or college. You have several options. You can put it in a piggy bank, or you can give it to the bank. The bank will pay you a fee, or interest, because they invest the money that they hold in order to make more money.

Bank Loans

Bank A offers a passbook savings account which will pay four percent interest if you leave the money in the account for a year. You can take the money out at any time, but you will not receive the full four percent interest if you do. The formula A = P + (P x R x T) is used to compute the value of the account at the end of the year. In this formula, A is the total amount at the end of the year, P is the principle or the starting amount, R is the percentage rate, and T is the length of time the money remains with the bank.

Bank B also offers a savings account at four percent interest. In this account, the interest is compounded or calculated quarterly (four times a year) and added to the principle. Each time the interest is calculated, the principle has increased. In this case, the formula for each quarter is A = P + (P x R x ¼).

Calculate and compare the interest paid in each of these accounts.

Savings Bonds

You may want to consider buying a United States Savings Bond. You may purchase a savings bond for 75 percent of the face value. Although you may cash the bond after three months, if you hold it for five years, it will then be worth the face value.

What face value can you purchase with your $100? If you hold it to maturity (5 years), what is the percent of interest it will earn?

Certificates of Deposits

Most banks also offer certificates of deposit, or CDs. A CD requires a minimum investment, usually $1,000. Unlike a passbook account, you must leave the money in the CD for a specified period of time, which can range from three months to several years. In general, the rates for a CD are higher than for a savings account.

Visit one or more local banks and gather information on their savings accounts and CDs. Make a chart to compare the different accounts. Be sure to note any other factors that should be considered, like minimum balance, minimum deposit, and service charges.

The Cookie Business

Everyone enjoys the cookies that you bake. To earn money, you decide to go into business for yourself by making and selling your cookies. Your mother said that you could use the kitchen and her baking equipment, but you will have to buy your own ingredients. Before you begin, you must make a business plan to see if this really is a good idea. Complete each of the following steps to create a business.

1	Who will buy your cookies? Create a questionnaire asking students, neighbors, and others if they would buy cookies from you. Ask what types of cookie they would buy, how much would they be willing to pay, and how many would they buy from you. Here is your first decision. Are there customers for your enterprise?
2	How much will it cost to make the cookies? After determining the types of cookies that the customers will buy, research the cost of making the cookies by going to the store and getting prices for the ingredients.
3	Add up the cost for all of the ingredients and divide by the number of cookies the recipe will make. How much does it cost to make each cookie? Subtract this amount from what your potential customers said that they would pay for the cookies. This is the amount of profit for each cookie sold. If all the cookies are sold, what would be the profit? What would it be if only $\frac{1}{2}$ of the cookies sold?
4	Now consider different scenarios. Should those who buy more than one cookie receive a discount? Should someone who wants to buy cookies every week receive a discount? Look at some of the ways other business people encourage customers to buy their products, and list some creative ideas for marketing the cookies.
5	If the plan looks good, it can be shown to people who might be willing to "invest" in the business or make a loan to get the business started. The plan will show that this is a serious and well thought out enterprise. Write your plan on another piece of paper, and if you are serious, you are on your way.

Buying a Car

The price of a new car varies according to a number of factors, including the size and the manufacturer. There is a base price for a car and a variety of optional features you may select for an additional cost. Some of these options come in a package, while others are priced individually. Research three different new cars you would like to own. Fill in the following grid by researching the newspaper and/or calling a car dealer.

model			
base price			
options			
total cost			

Most people finance their cars. This means that they take out a loan for part or all of the cost of the car. The loan is repaid over a period of three to five years. Interest must also be paid on the loan. Choose one of the cars above and complete the chart below to find out what the new car will actually cost in each of the following scenarios:

1. You traded your old car for $5,000 and are taking a loan for the balance at 13 percent for 3 years.

2. This is your first car, and you have $3,000 to put down. The difference will be financed at 11 percent for five years.

3. This is your first car, and you have no money to put down. Finance the total cost of the car over five years at 18 percent interest. (You are a high risk here.)

Calculate the actual cost and complete the chart below.

Scenarios	1	2	3
cost of new car			
down payment			
amount financed			
percentage rate			
length of loan			
total cost			

The Pyramid Scheme

This was a very popular idea in the 1980s. Here is how it works. One person is number 1. That person finds two friends and says, "You go find two people each. Ask them to invest $200 each. You keep one half and give me one half. Once they have invested, ask each of them to find two new investors. They will keep 25 percent of what they receive and give you the rest. You will keep 25 percent and give me the remaining 50 percent. We will start this and let it keep going."

Here is a schematic representation:

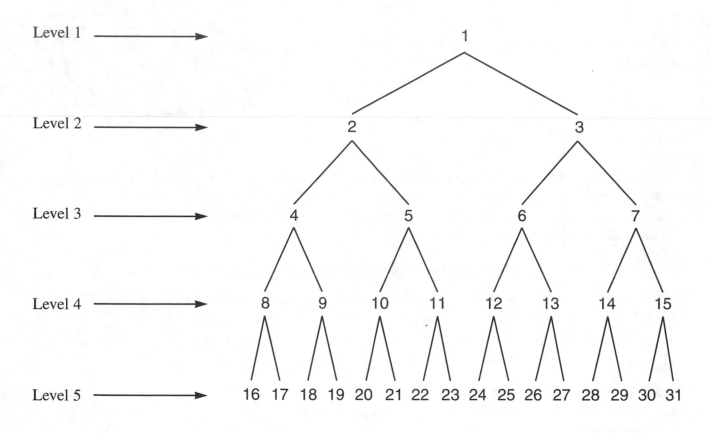

Use the information above to complete the following problems:

1. Notice the first three people did not have to put out any money. They just started the pyramid. Did they each get the same amount of money?

2. At level three, the individual keeps 25 percent of any money he or she receives. How many levels will it take before he or she makes back the original investment?

3. When level 6 joins the pyramid, how much would each higher level expect to make?